To Know
As We Are Known

WITHDRAWN

OTHER BOOKS BY PARKER J. PALMER

The Active Life: Wisdom for Work, Creativity, and Caring

The Company of Strangers: Christians and the Renewal of America's Public Life

The Promise of Paradox: A Celebration of Contradictions in the Christian Life

TO KNOW
AS WE ARE KNOWN

Education as a Spiritual Journey

PARKER J. PALMER

 HarperSanFrancisco
A Division of HarperCollins*Publishers*

Designer: Jim Mennick

FIRST HARPERCOLLINS PAPERBACK EDITION PUBLISHED IN 1993

Library of Congress Cataloging-in-Publication Data

Palmer, Parker J.
　　To know as we are known : a spirituality of education / Parker J. Palmer.
　　　p.　cm.
　　Originally published: San Francisco : Harper & Row, 1983. With new introduction.
　　Includes bibliographical references and index.
　　ISBN 0–06–066451–7
　　1. Palmer, Parker J.　2. Education—Philosophy.　3. Spiritual life.
I. Title.
LB885.P34T6　　　1993
370'.1—dc20　　　　　　　　　　　　　　　　　　　　　92–54712

---

01 00 99　　RRD(H)　　20 19 18 17

For Brent and Todd and Carrie

Contents

Preface for the Paperback Edition

The Recovery of Community in Education

The Hidden Wholeness

Ten years ago, when this book was first published, I thought I knew who my readers would be—faculty at church-related colleges and seminaries, professors of religion, and people involved in religious education. After all, the book is about the spiritual dimension of education, and conventional wisdom tells us that educators range from indifferent to cynical on matters of the spirit.

But now, I am delighted that *To Know as We Are Known* has reached a wider and more diverse audience than I had thought possible. Today, I spend half my time on the road, exploring the issues in this book with faculty at public schools and state universities, at independent colleges and major research institutions—faculty who are Jewish or Muslim or Buddhist or who have no formal religious identity. Grateful as I am for my continuing conversation with educators in church-related settings, this dialogue amid diversity has enlarged and enriched my thinking.

Why has a book about the spirituality of education, written from a Christian viewpoint, reached such a pluralistic audience? I hope it is partly because this book offers a spirituality that respects other traditions and is eager to learn from them. But I know there is a more basic explanation: educators of all sorts are in real pain these days, and that pain has compelled them to explore unconventional resources.

When suffering becomes intense, we are forced to examine the deeper dimensions of our condition and to consider sources of insight that may have seemed uncouth when we and our world were humming with power and success. The teachers I meet have no illusions that education is "working." They know that students are often served poorly in the classroom, and that their own growth as teachers is not supported by the system. They are weary of their profession's tendency to seek shallow technical "fixes" for complex human problems. They are ready to look beyond technique for whatever guidance may come from spiritual traditions.

I call the pain that permeates education "the pain of disconnection." Everywhere I go, I meet faculty who feel disconnected from their colleagues, from their students, and from their own hearts. Most of us go into teaching not for fame or fortune but because of a passion to connect. We feel deep kinship with some subject; we want to bring students into that relationship, to link them with the knowledge that is so life-giving to us; we want to work in community with colleagues who share our values and our vocation. But when institutional conditions create more combat than community, when the life of the mind alienates more than it connects, the heart goes out of things, and there is little left to sustain us.

In the midst of such pain, the spiritual traditions offer hope that is hard to find elsewhere, for all of them are ultimately concerned with getting us reconnected. These traditions build on the great truth that beneath the broken surface of our lives there remains—in the words of Thomas Merton—"a hidden wholeness." The hope of every wisdom tradition is to recall us to that wholeness in the midst of our torn world, to reweave us into the community that is so threadbare today. That, I think, is why the spirituality of education is now being explored in so many "unlikely" places. Perhaps the ancient communal act called teaching and learning can be renewed by drawing upon spiritual wisdom.

But if the spiritual traditions have wisdom to offer, we who speak for them have often spoken unwisely. I admire the patience of those secular educators who are still willing to explore issues in spirituality, for the sad fact is that past marriages of religion and education have done education at least as much harm as good. Too often, the spiritual traditions have been used to obstruct inquiry rather than encourage it. Too often, would-be educators who profess religious faith turn out to fear truth, rather than welcome it in all its forms.

That is why I devoted this book to a spirituality of "sources" in education rather than one of "ends." A spirituality of ends wants to dictate the desirable outcomes of education in the life of the student. It uses the spiritual tradition as a template against which the ideas, beliefs, and behaviors of the student are to be measured. The goal is to shape the student to the template by the time his or her formal education concludes.

But that sort of education never gets started; it is no education at all. Authentic spirituality wants to open us to truth—whatever truth may be, wherever truth may take us. Such a spirituality does not dictate where we must go, but trusts that any path walked with integrity will take us to a place of knowledge. Such a spirituality encourages us to welcome diversity and conflict, to tolerate ambiguity, and to embrace paradox. By this understanding, the spirituality of education is not about dictating ends. It is about examining and clarifying the inner sources of teaching and learning, ridding us of the toxins that poison our hearts and minds.

For example, an authentic spirituality of education will address the fear that so often permeates and destroys teaching and learning. It will understand that fear, not ignorance, is the enemy of learning, and that fear is what gives ignorance its power. It will try to root out our fear of having our ignorance exposed and our orthodoxies challenged—whether those orthodoxies are religious or secular. A spirituality of education will ground us in the confidence that our search for truth, and truth's search for us, can lead to new life beyond the death of our half-truths and narrow concepts.

The Community of Truth

My encounters with diverse educators over the past decade have led me to reformulate one of the images central to this book. In Chapters 5 and 6, I suggest that "to teach is to create a space in which obedience to truth is practiced." Because that image is crucial to my notion of authentic education, I have been distressed to discover that some people are unable to explore it openly because they distrust the idea of "obedience."

Although I tried, in the book, to rescue "obedience" from its authoritarian connotations, I understand why some people resist the word. For African-Americans, women, young people, and other historically marginalized people, the notion of "obedience" has too often been used to keep them "in their place" and to justify unjust power. "Obey *whose* truth?" is the question they always ask me—and despite my answer, "The one that emerges between us," our dialogue often gets derailed. Because I believe that the gift of language should be used to bridge our gaps, not widen them, I wanted to find a more inclusive way to say what I meant by "practicing obedience to truth."

Several years ago, I found a phrase that is faithful to my original intent, but that stimulates rather than stops conversation: "To teach is to create a space in which the community of truth is practiced." This "community of truth" is what I originally meant by "obedience"—a rich and complex network of relationships in which we must both speak and listen, make claims on others, and make ourselves accountable. This new image makes it easier to explore with others the pain of disconnection, and to seek remedies consistent with the nature of education at its best.

Because the pain of disconnection has become so severe, there is more talk today then there was ten years ago about the recovery of community in education. If that talk is to bear fruit, we need to use images of community consistent with the aims of education, which I take to be *knowing, teaching,* and *learning.* "The community of truth" should be our goal. Unfortunately, the discussion about community in education is seldom framed in this way. Instead, we borrow communal images from other realms, impose them on education, and then wonder why we get so much friction and such a poor fit.

For example, as I listen to the conversation about community in education, the image I most often hear propounded is one of "therapeutic community." Therapeutic community requires a capacity for open, vulnerable relationships so that psychological wounds can be revealed and healed; in this image, community equals intimacy. Is intimacy a good thing, a valuable form of relationship? Of course. Is it the kind of community best suited to the aims of education? I think not. While knowing, teaching, and learning require intimacy in certain forms, education would be distorted if intimacy became its ultimate norm.

Another image prominent in the conversation about community in education is that of "civic community." Civic community is not about intimacy; it is about the relations of strangers who will never know each other well, but who must learn to hang together lest they hang separately. The goal of such a community is to learn how to compromise, and the norm for relationships within that community is one of tolerance and civility. Is civility a good thing, a valuable form of relationship? Of course. Is it the kind of community best suited to the aims of education? I think not. While knowing, teaching, and learning require civility in certain forms, education would be distorted if civility became its ultimate norm.

Rather than borrow images from other realms of experience, we need to draw an image of community from the world of education, of knowing and teaching and learning. When we tap our own sources, we will find a heartening fact: at the frontiers of intellectual life, scholars now regard the concept of community as indispensable in describing the terrain that educators inhabit.

Community is clearly central to four issues that have long been basic to the life of the mind: the nature of reality (ontology), how we know reality (epistemology), how we teach and learn (pedagogy), and how education forms or deforms our lives in the world (ethics). Under these rubrics, I offer some notes toward a recovery of community that is both appropriate to the world of education and rooted in a spiritual understanding of "the hidden wholeness."

Communal Images of Reality and How We Know It

The Nature of Reality

Since the advent of atomic physics, the popular image of physical reality has been one of particles floating in an empty void. Since Darwin and Social Darwinism, the popular image of biological reality has been one of individual creatures in bloody competition over scarce resources, of "nature red in tooth and claw" (Tennyson). Though they come from different disciplines, these two images of reality share an important trait: they are essentially non-communal, even anti-communal.

But at the heart of science itself, these images have been challenged and changed. Community, not competition, is the metaphor that most deeply informs the work of many biologists. Among physicists, the atom is no longer seen as an independent and isolated entity, but, in the words of Henry Stapp, as "a set of relationships reaching out to other things." So Thomas Merton's "hidden wholeness" turns out to be more than a spiritual fantasy—the connections of community are visible at reality's very core.

These might be no more than arcane abstractions were it not for the fact the our culture and institutions tend to take shape around our dominant metaphors of reality, and to hold that shape long after our metaphors have changed. Just as ancient China ordered its social life around a cosmology of interdependence, so modern America has fashioned itself around a cosmology of fragmentation. For over a century, atomism, individualism, and competition have been institutionalized in our society and in our schools. Modern physicists may have abandoned the image of atoms floating in the void, but we still have a culture of individualism which mirrors that discredited worldview. Modern biologists may have abandoned images of bloody competition, but we still have schools that offer students an education that is "red in tooth and claw."

What if we overcame this cultural lag and reformed education around the images of contemporary science? We know that students learn as much from the "hidden curriculum" of institutional patterns and practices as from the formal curriculum of concepts and facts, so education would be more truthful if our schools themselves became more reflective of the communal nature of the realities we teach in school. Students would learn more true lessons about the nature of life on all levels if we were to shape our schools around images of reality that are less individualistic and competitive, and more cooperative and communal.

How We Know Reality

We can find this communal theme not only in modern images of the nature of reality, but also in modern images of how reality is known. In the popular imagination, knowing is seen as the act of a solitary individual, a knower who uses sense and intellect to apprehend and interpret objects of knowledge "out there." Not only does this knower operate apart from other knowers, he or she is also set apart from the known object in order to guarantee that our knowledge will be "objective" and pure. The popular image of how we know reality is as non- or anti-communal as is the popular image of the nature of reality itself.

But scholars now understand that knowing is a profoundly communal act. Nothing could possibly be known by the solitary self, since the self is inherently communal in nature. In order to know something, we depend on the consensus of the community in which we are rooted—a consensus so deep that we often draw upon it unconsciously. For example, the scientific community agrees that reality consists of that which is available to our senses. It does not matter that all of us, including scientists, depend on realities that our senses cannot detect. No scientist would introduce extrasensory factors into a research report—unless that scientist was willing to risk his or her communal membership.

The communal nature of knowing goes beyond the relations of knowers; it includes a community of interaction between knowers and the known. The myth of objectivity, which depends on a radical separation of the knower from the known, has been declared bankrupt. We now see that to know something is to have a living relationship with it—influencing and being influenced by the object known. When Fritjof Capra says, "We can never speak of nature without, at the same time, speaking about ourselves," the death knell of objectivism has been sounded.

These communal images of knowing show that the mind is not the disconnective faculty portrayed by objectivism. Anyone who loves to think knows that the mind can connect us more deeply to ourselves and to the world. A historian thinks about the "dead" past in order to reveal our relationship with a past that lives in us. A biologist, thinking about "voiceless" nature, gives us ears to hear what nature has to say. The true work of the mind is to reconnect us with that which would otherwise be out of reach, to reweave the great community of our lives.

There is a simple reason why some students resist thinking: they live in a world where relationships are often quite fragile. They are desperate for more community, not less, so when thinking is presented to them as a way of disconnecting themselves from each other and from the world, they want nothing of it. If we could represent knowing for what it is—a way of creating community, not destroying it—we would draw more young people into the great adventure of learning.

Communal Images of Teaching, Learning, and Living

How We Teach and Learn

A third area in which scholars are rediscovering the centrality of community is pedagogy, theories of how we teach and learn. It is no surprise that our dominant images of teaching and learning are individualistic and competitive rather than communal; they are derived from images of reality and of knowing that bear these same marks. If reality consists of atoms in the void or individuals in competition, and if knowing consists of gathering discrete data about objects, then teaching and learning will mean delivering data to students who must compete for those scarce rewards called grades.

But what scholars now say—and what good teachers have always known—is that real learning does not happen until students are brought into relationship with the teacher, with each other, and with the subject. We cannot learn deeply and well until a community of learning is created in the classroom.

It is no accident that communal images of pedagogy are being recovered even as communal images of epistemology are being reclaimed. The way we teach depends on the way we think people know; we cannot amend our pedagogy until our epistemology is transformed. If teaching is reformed in our time, it will not be the result of snappier teaching techniques. It will happen because we are in the midst of a far-reaching intellectual and spiritual revisioning of reality and how we know it.

We do not learn best by memorizing facts about the subject. Because reality is communal, we learn best by interacting with it. In the practical disciplines, this may mean working with materials, creating artifacts, and solving problems. In the more abstract disciplines, it may mean learning how scholars generate, criticize, and use the concepts and data of their fields. In a wide variety of ways, good teachers bring students into living communion with the subjects they teach.

Good teachers also bring students into community with themselves and with each other—not simply for the sake of warm feelings, but to do the difficult things that teaching and learning require. The debate over educational reform has often been polarized between the apostles of the "hard" intellectual virtues and the disciples of the "soft" emotional virtues. It has been a fruitless debate because it has missed a simple point: the practice of intellectual rigor in the classroom requires an ethos of trust and acceptance. Intellectual rigor depends on things like honest dissent and the willingness to change our minds, things that will not happen if the "soft" values of community are lacking. In the absence of the communal virtues, intellectual rigor too easily turns into intellectual *rigor mortis*.

How We Live in the World

The vision of a communal classroom in which students learn by interacting with the subject and with each other leads to a fourth area in which community is being rediscovered—the ethics of education. Here, the central question is whether we are educating students in ways that make them responsive to the claims of community upon their lives. Are they simply learning to compete for scarce rewards as isolated individuals, or are they learning how to create communities of abundance in their lives both as learners and as citizens?

When we deal with ethics in education (and often we ignore it altogether), we approach it as a matter of helping individuals develop standards for personal behavior. Not only do we stress personal at the expense of communal ethics; deeper still, we ignore the fact that the presence, or absence, of communal imagery at every level of teaching and learning can form, or deform, students for life in the world. We underestimate the hidden curriculum of ethics that is being taught in classrooms even—and perhaps especially—when ethics is not the formal topic.

If we teach students to think of reality as a collection of atoms to be rearranged at our convenience, we are teaching an anti-community ethic. If we teach students to think of intellect as a tool for distancing and disconnecting ourselves from the world, we are teaching an anti-community ethic. If we teach students to compete for grades as if knowledge itself were a scarce commodity, we are teaching an anti-community ethic. When these things are taught in the hidden curriculum of images and practices, the content of the formal curriculum makes little difference—no matter how "communal" or "ethical" it may be.

Ultimately, an ethical education is one that creates a capacity for connectedness in the lives of students. Education has always been defined as the development of certain capacities (for example, critical thinking and the tolerance of ambiguity) that allow the educated person to live more productively and more at peace in a complex and demanding world. But these vital capacities are sometimes taught in ways that break community rather than build it. Critical thinking becomes a tool for disengagement, and tolerance of ambiguity becomes cheap relativism.

It need not be this way. Critical thinking can be taught as a mode of citizen participation, and tolerance of ambiguity can be taught as a way of listening to others without losing one's voice. But if community is not a foundation stone of the educational enterprise, these skills quickly degenerate into the capacity for disconnectedness that is so characteristic of educated people today.

At this crucial moment, we have an opportunity to revision education as a communal enterprise from the foundations up—in our images of reality, in our modes of knowing, in our ways of teaching and learning. Such a revisioning would result in a deeply ethical education, an education that would help students develop the capacity for connectedness that is at the heart of an ethical life.

Such an education would root ethics in its true and only ground, in the spiritual insight that beyond the broken surface of our lives there is a "hidden wholeness" on which all life depends. In such an education, intellect and spirit would be one, teachers and learners and subjects would be in vital community with one another, and a world in need of healing would be well served. That, finally, is the reason why the spirituality of education deserves and demands our attention.

Acknowledgments

This book began in 1978 when Henri Nouwen, John Mogab-gab, and I started a series of conversations on spirituality, community, and education. For two years we spent a day together every other week, talking, praying, laughing, and eating woefully inadequate lunches. Between meetings each of us wrote a brief essay in response to the preceding conversation; those essays then provided the starting point for our next meeting. So this book, which stresses the spiritual and communal dimensions of education, had its own origins in a small community of friendship, inquiry, and worship. My gratitude to Henri and John is great. In their generosity of mind and heart this book took its birth.

In 1980–81, a Fellowship in the Institute for Ecumenical and Cultural Research at St. John's University and Abbey gave me the opportunity to complete a first draft. I am grateful to the staff and Fellows of the Institute for their stimulation and encouragement. I am also indebted to Robert W. Lynn and other staff of the Lilly Endowment Inc., for the financial support that helped this work along.

Several people have criticized portions and versions of the manuscript. I am grateful to Robert W. Lynn, Sally Palmer, Robert Rankin, Peg Stearn, and Barbara G. Wheeler for their caring and challenging response to my words. My editor at Harper & Row, John Shopp, not only helped clarify the purposes and structure of the book but supported me through a period of discouragement. My copyeditor, Ann Moru, helped considerably to sharpen my prose. My thanks also go to Patricia DiFabio, who managed to type a clean and crisp final draft from my sometimes illegible scrawl.

Because this book is critical of much education, including parts of my own, I want to express my gratitude to those teachers I met along the way who offered me models of another way to teach and learn. Robert N. Bellah, Robert McAfee Brown, William L. Kolb, David Maitland, Charles McCoy, Bardwell Smith, and Steve Stalonas are among those who have been my guides toward a way of educating that joins the mind with the heart.

Finally, my gratitude goes to the people of Pendle Hill, a Quaker community and adult study center where I have lived and worked these past ten years. In this place, with these people, my search for a spirituality of education has been given a depth and a direction it would otherwise have lacked.

Introduction

But yield who will to their separation,
My object in living is to unite
My avocation and my vocation
As my two eyes make one in sight.
                              —Robert Frost

Many of us live one-eyed lives. We rely largely on the eye of
the mind to form our image of reality. But today more and more
of us are opening the other eye, the eye of the heart, looking for
realities to which the mind's eye is blind. Either eye alone is not
enough. We need "wholesight," a vision of the world in which
mind and heart unite "as my two eyes make one in sight." Our
seeing shapes our being. Only as we see whole can we and our
world be whole.

With the mind's eye we see a world of fact and reason. It is a
cold and mechanical place, but we have built our lives there
because it seemed predictable and safe. Today, in the age of nuclear science, our mind-made world has been found flawed and
dangerous, even lethal. So we open the eye of the heart and see
another sight: a world warmed and transformed by the power of
love, a vision of community beyond the mind's capacity to see.
We cannot forsake our hearts and yet we cannot abandon our
minds. How shall we bring together these two lines of sight?
How shall we use both eyes to create not a blurry double image
but one world, in all its dimensions, healed and made whole?
This book is my attempt at an answer.

My vocation (to use the poet's term) is the spiritual life, the
quest for God, which relies on the eye of the heart. My avocation
is education, the quest for knowledge, which relies on the eye of
the mind. I have seen life through both these eyes as long as I

can remember—but the two images have not always coincided. Sometimes I have struggled with the spiritual crisis brought on by the educated mind: how can the heart be true when my senses and reason reduce reality so self-confidently to their own narrow terms? Sometimes the question has turned: how can these diminishments of reality possibly be credited when the spiritual vision is so rich with depth and meaning? But—unable to blink one eye, shut them both, or live in a blur—I have been forced to find ways for my eyes to work together, to find a common focus for my spirit-seeking heart and my knowledge-seeking mind that embraces reality in all its amazing dimensions.

The search for "wholesight," for rounder ways of knowing reality, is on in earnest today. My vision has been sharpened by several recent probes that show that knowing draws not only on our senses and our reason, but on our intuitions, our beliefs, our actions, our relationships, and on our bodies themselves. I am thinking especially of the philosophy of science that builds on the findings of the new physics, of feminist insights that emerge as women articulate their way of being in the world, and of inquiries into Native American and other aboriginal ways of knowing.

In this book I hope to contribute to "wholesight" from another angle of vision, one found at the heart of my spiritual tradition. The mind's vision excludes the heart, but the heart's vision can include the mind. I believe that my spiritual tradition offers a viewpoint from which the two eyes can see—single, steady, and whole.

In this secular age, with religion on the wrong side of the fact-fantasy divide, it may seem odd to turn to spirituality for a new way of knowing. I do so because I am ultimately concerned not only with knowledge but with truth. Most academic disciplines have largely abandoned truth in favor of facts and reasons; spirituality is the one discipline I know still committed to compassing truth in the round. Perhaps this book will interest people for whom truth is an intellectual issue. I hope even more that it will speak to people for whom truth is the fabric of daily life.

My spirituality is Christian, so I trust that this book will be useful to other Christians who are concerned with the life and limits of the mind. But I also hope it will speak to people of other religious traditions, that they will find in my treatment of Christian themes not mere tolerance but affirmation of their spiritual visions.

Because education is my avocation, my quest for a holistic way of knowing must be translated into practical ways to teach and to learn. I hope that this book will be helpful to teachers and students seeking unity of vision in their own work. But I hope, too, that it will be useful to any ex-student who wants to expand the one-eyed view of things education tends to give us.

I am asking a series of impossible questions, of course. What is truth? How can I know truth? How can I teach truth? One does not "answer" such questions in any conventional sense. But I know of no better way to keep my knowing, my teaching, and myself alive than to keep the vision of truth continually before me, to look sharp with both eyes, however blurred the vision at first may be, and to respond to what I see, however risky my response may feel. I invite you to join me in that seeing and that seeking and to let me join you in the ancient and ever new encounter of the human soul with the spirit of truth.

In Chapter 1 I ask where modern knowledge is taking us. I reflect on my own education and where it has taken me, reflections that help me understand some troubling data about where the present generation of students is headed. In the process, I uncover a prior question: where does our knowledge come from? The answer comes from the heart of my spiritual tradition, so in this chapter I lay a groundwork for "a spirituality of education."

In Chapter 2 I show how standard education forms—or deforms—our seeing and our being. After exploring some of the formative disciplines employed by education, I find the source of our deformation in the "objectivist" theory of knowing that dominates most education today. Since objectivism is not sustained by our best contemporary philosophical reflection, I ask where it comes from, and argue that it is an outcome of our conventional methods of teaching.

In Chapter 3 I analyze those methods and describe their impact on students. After asking why this mode of teaching is so widespread and tenacious, despite many efforts at reform, I tell a story about another way to teach and learn—a fourth century tale from the desert fathers and mothers who founded the monastic movement and are a root-source of Christian spiritual tradition.

In Chapter 4 I explore the image of truth at the heart of that tradition, the image of a person who said "I am . . . the truth" and who invited all who wished to know truth into a community of faithful relationships. I spell out some implications of this personal and communal conception of truth—not only for religious knowledge, but for our knowledge in physical science, social science, and the humanities.

In Chapters 5 and 6 I describe some practical ways of teaching and learning that flow from this way of knowing. Here I suggest that "to teach is to create a space in which obedience to truth is practiced." Chapter 5 asks how the teacher can create a space for learning. Chapter 6 asks how teachers and students can practice obedience to truth within that space.

In Chapter 7 I explore the spiritual disciplines necessary to do that kind of teaching. If we teachers are to help form our students in the image of truth, we must attend to our own re-formation. Having had our vision shaped by one-eyed education, and working under conditions that discourage us from opening the other eye, we are in special need of exercises that can help us see and be whole.

1. Knowing Is Loving

The Violence of Our Knowledge

> I have felt it myself. The glitter of nuclear weapons. It is irresistible if you come to them as a scientist. To feel it's there in your hands—to release the energy that fuels the stars. To let it do your bidding. To perform these miracles—to lift a million tons of rock into the sky. It is something that gives people an illusion of illimitable power and it is, in some ways, responsible for all our troubles, I would say—this what you might call technical arrogance that overcomes people when they see what they can do with their minds.[1]

These words were spoken by a celebrated physicist in *The Day after Trinity*, a film documentary about the team of American scientists who produced the first atomic bomb. "Trinity" was the ironic code name for that original explosion, and only on "the day after" did the scientists stop to analyze and agonize over the outcomes of their work.

The film is filled with images of horror. For me, the most horrifying is not that mushroom shape that appears in our dreams and lurks just over our waking horizon. Instead, it is the image of intelligent and educated people—the most intelligent and the best educated our society has produced—devoting themselves so enthusiastically to such demonic ends. They appear in the film as people possessed by a power beyond their control—not the power of the government that summoned their services, but the power of their knowledge itself. One scientist interviewed in the film reveals that "prior to the shot, back in the lab, there had been some speculation that it might be possible to explode the atmosphere—in which case the world disappears."[2] But the "experiment" went on as scheduled, the irresistible outcome of the knowledge that made it possible.

Watching this film, reliving that history, I saw how our knowledge can carry us toward ends we want to renounce—but we renounce them only on "the day after." I understood then what Jonathan Schell says in *The Fate of the Earth:* "It is fundamental to the shape and character of the nuclear predicament that its origins lie in scientific knowledge rather than in social circumstances."[3] I understood, too, what Robert Oppenheimer meant in his post-Hiroshima pronouncement, "The physicists have known sin."

We need images of hope to counteract our horror, knowledge of grace to counteract our knowledge of sin. That is what I want to offer in this book by describing a way of knowing and educating that might heal rather than wound us and our world. But in my spiritual life I have learned that hope and grace do not come cheap. They require honest self-scrutiny first, and then confession, an offering up of our own inner darkness to the source of forgiveness and transformation.

I am not a nuclear physicist, and I have never participated in a project with such vast implications as "Trinity," but I identify with those scientists. Their story is my story too, and when I am tempted to sit in judgment on them I am only evading the judgment that falls upon me. I value their confession of sin on a large scale because it helps me make my own confession of smaller but similar sins.

For all the differences between those scientists and me, we have one thing in common. We are well-educated people who have been schooled in a way of knowing that treats the world as an object to be dissected and manipulated, a way of knowing that gives us power over the world. With those scientists I have succumbed to the arrogance that comes when we see what our minds can do. The outcomes of my arrogance have been less than world-shaking because my powers are small. But in my own way I have used my knowledge to rearrange the world to satisfy my drive for power, distorting and deranging life rather than loving it for the gift it is.

In my late twenties, still impressed by what I could do with my mind, I wrote a book about how we know the world around us. (By grace, that book was never published—not, I suspect, be-

cause it was wrongheaded, but because my wrongheadedness
was not packaged well enough to sell.) The themes of that book
may sound distant and abstract, but bear with me for a moment:
I want to show how they shaped the way one educated person
used his knowledge and lived his life.

In that book I argued that knowledge emerges as we impose a
mental order on the chaos that surrounds us. The world, I said,
presents itself to us as nothing more than a welter of sensory
impressions—colors, tastes, smells, and textures; weights,
heights, and lengths. To make sense of this chaos we use concepts to organize our impressions and theories to organize our
concepts. The test of truth for any one of these mental constructs
is simply how well it fits the data and helps us solve the intellectual or practical problem at hand.

Not only did my book imply that the world has no necessary
shape or order of its own; it also suggested that the shape im-
posed on the world by our minds has no validity outside of a
culture that happens to find that pattern congenial. Christians
and Zen Buddhists, scientists and artists have different ways of
ordering the world because they live in different cultures and
have different problems to solve. By my scheme, knowing becomes an arbitrary process, subject only to the rules of whatever
culture-game one happens to be playing at the time.

Looking back, I see how my theory of knowing helped form
(or deform) my sense of who I was and how I was related to the
world. For many years I regarded thinking as a kind of board
game in which we move the pieces around until we have solved
the problem, placing the pieces in patterns that allow us to
"win." "Winning" meant different things in different settings,
according to different rules. For a while, my setting was school.
Here, the winning pattern of pieces was whatever the professors
were willing to reward with high grades. Truth was reduced to
whatever would give me an "A." As I moved into professional
academic life, winning meant arranging the pieces in ways ac-
ceptable to my peers. Now the criteria of truth became publication in professional journals and academic appointments and ad-

vancements. When I left the academy to go into community organizing, truth was weighed by its ability to help me win the political battle at hand. My ethic was opportunistic, dictated by the demands of the situation—an ethic that reflected the manipulative mode of knowing described in that stillborn book, where "truth" is whatever works.

Watching *The Day after Trinity* I saw that same ethic, that same mode of knowing at work. I also saw, projected on a very large screen, the violence wrought by this way of knowing and living. In my own life, the dimensions of that violence eventually became clear. I was distanced and alienated from the world around me; too many parts of it became pawns in my game, valued only for how they might help me win. I worked toward shaping that world in my own image. Sometimes I succeeded—but the results were only temporarily pleasing, since the image in which I was shaping things was that of a distorted, driven self. Sometimes I failed, since the world does not always yield—then the results were anger and even more violent efforts at compelling the world to change. The ultimate outcome for me was growing weariness, withdrawal, and cynicism. What else could result from a way of knowing and living driven mainly by the need for power and deficient in the capacity to love?

A recent Carnegie Commission survey of American undergraduates suggests that my story is not unique.[4] The study reveals that these best-educated of our young men and women are darkly pessimistic about the future of their country and their world. They are, among other things, "fearful of the economy, pollution, crime, morals, energy, and nuclear war." But at the same time they are brightly optimistic about their personal futures. They believe that the knowledge they have gained through education—especially with the access it gives them to their professions—will enable them to carve out a niche of private safety and sanity in the midst of public calamity. They believe, as I once did, that they can "win" while everyone around them is losing.

The researchers cite this interview as typical:

> *Interviewer:* Will the United States be a better or worse place to live in the next ten years?
>
> *Student:* The U.S. will definitely be a worse place to live.
>
> *Interviewer:* Then you must be pessimistic about the future?
>
> *Student:* No, I'm optimistic.
>
> *Interviewer* (with surprise): Why?
>
> *Student:* Because I have a high grade point average, and I'm going to get a good job, make a lot of money, and live in a nice house.[5]

There are various ways to interpret these findings. A psychiatrist might call these students schizophrenic; by clinging to a fantasy of private well-being, they shield themselves from overwhelming public horrors. A liberal arts teacher would see their answers as evidence that vocationalism has replaced education's historic goal of helping us see and think clearly. But my own experience suggests that their fantastic ethic reflects the mode of knowing in which they have been schooled. They have learned that the world is an object to be manipulated, and though they have lost my generation's confidence that the whole world can be rearranged, they still believe that a small part of it can be organized to suit their personal needs.

Conventional wisdom will bemoan the fact that these well-trained men and women have turned their backs on the world and are unlikely to use their knowledge to help solve its problems. But many of the problems these students fear and flee from (notably the nuclear threat) were created by their well-educated predecessors. The respondents to the Carnegie survey all grew up on "the day after Trinity"; they are victims of a kind of knowing that begins and ends in human pride and power. Since this is the same kind of knowing in which these students themselves have been formed, we must wonder whether those who refuse to flee but decide to engage the world will not in turn become the victimizers of the next generation.

The Trinity scientists, the Carnegie students, and I—each of us

overcome by the arrogance of our knowledge, each of us inflict-
ing that arrogance on the common life. Such, at least, is my confession, a confession that other educated men and women may
wish to share. But confession is only a first step in the spiritual
life, my first step toward a spirituality of education that might
yield a knowledge that can heal, not wound, the world. As we
pray for grace and hope, we must try to understand more about
the knowledge we possess; for that knowledge also possesses us.

The Origins and Ends of Knowledge

The ends of knowledge has been a subject of much earnest and
worried talk in recent years. We have celebrated the powers of
the human mind in our century, reveled in the far-reaching advances of science. But now we begin to wonder where all this
knowledge is taking us. We worry about the ecological consequences of technology, about the power of applied social science
to manipulate human behavior, about the grotesque potentials of
genetic engineering, and above all about the translation of nuclear physics into instruments of oblivion. Is our knowledge—the
very knowledge that distinguishes human beings from the
beasts—creating a world far less human, far more beastly, than
the natural world itself?

The question is urgent, and the evidence in response to it is
troubling. But the problem will not have been truly engaged until
we ask about the *origins* of our knowledge as well as its ends.
Where does our knowledge come from? What is its ultimate
source? What is the wellspring of our passion to know?

We have ignored the question of origins because we imagine
that knowledge begins as neutral stuff—"the facts." Facts are
facts, we say, and we can neither alter them nor stop gathering
them. The problem, we believe, is not how our knowledge arises
but how we use and apply those neutral facts. We think that
knowledge itself is passionless and purposeless. So our strategy
for guiding its course is to surround the facts with ethics, moral
mandates meant to control the passions and purposes of those

who use the facts—the engineers, the industrialists, the politicians. It is a strategy now employed by our schools where the occasional course in "values" is offered as a supplement to the standard factual fare.

But I have come to see that knowledge contains its own morality, that it begins not in a neutrality but in a place of passion within the human soul. Depending on the nature of that passion, our knowledge will follow certain courses and head toward certain ends. From the point where it originates in the soul, knowledge assumes a certain trajectory and target—and it will not easily be deflected by ethics once it takes off from that source. In a day when nuclear missiles have become ominous symbols of our knowledge, "trajectory" and "target" are apt images. If we are worried about the path on which our knowledge flies and about its ultimate destination, we had better go back to its launching pad and deal with the passions that fuel and guide its course.

History suggests two primary sources for our knowledge, both of which are evident on "the day after Trinity." One is curiosity; the other is control. The one corresponds to pure, speculative knowledge, to knowledge as an end in itself. The other corresponds to applied science, to knowledge as a means to practical ends.

We are inquisitive creatures, forever wanting to get inside of things and discover their hidden secrets. Our curiosity is piqued by the closed and wrapped box. We want to know its contents, and when the contents are out we want to open them too—down to the tiniest particle of their construction. We are also creatures attracted by power; we want knowledge to control our environment, each other, ourselves. Since many of the boxes we have opened contained secrets that have given us more mastery over life, curiosity and control are joined as the passion behind our knowing.

Curiosity sometimes kills, and our desire to control has put deadly power in some very unsteady hands. We should not be surprised that knowledge launched from these sources is heading toward some terrible ends, undeflected by ethical values as basic as respect for life itself. Curiosity is an amoral passion, a need to know that allows no guidance beyond the need itself. Control is simply another word for power, a passion notorious not only for its amorality but for its tendency toward corruption. If curiosity and control are the primary motives for our knowing, we will generate a knowledge that eventually carries us not toward life but death.

But another kind of knowledge is available to us, one that begins in a different passion and is drawn toward other ends. This knowledge can contain as much sound fact and theory as the knowledge we now possess, but because it springs from a truer passion it works toward truer ends. This is a knowledge that originates not in curiosity or control but in compassion, or love—a source celebrated not in our intellectual tradition but in our spiritual heritage.

The goal of a knowledge arising from love is the reunification and reconstruction of broken selves and worlds. A knowledge born of compassion aims not at exploiting and manipulating creation but at reconciling the world to itself. The mind motivated by compassion reaches out to know as the heart reaches out to love. Here, the act of knowing *is* an act of love, the act of entering and embracing the reality of the other, of allowing the other to enter and embrace our own. In such knowing we know and are known as members of one community, and our knowing becomes a way of reweaving that community's bonds.

Our spiritual heritage does not merely claim that knowing *ought* to begin in love, though surely it should. But that claim is mere exhortation, another futile attempt to deflect the course of knowledge by battering it with "oughts." Our spiritual tradition makes a deeper and more substantial claim: the origin of knowledge *is* love. The deepest wellspring of our desire to know is the passion to recreate the organic community in which the world was first created.

The minds we have used to divide and conquer creation were given to us for another purpose: to raise to awareness the communal nature of reality, to overcome separateness and alienation by a knowing that *is* loving, to reach out with intelligence to acknowledge and renew the bonds of life. The failure of modern knowledge is not primarily a failure in our ethics, in the application of what we know. Rather, it is the failure of our knowing itself to recognize and reach for its deeper source and passion, to allow love to inform the relations that our knowledge creates— with ourselves, with each other, with the whole animate and inanimate world.

This love is not a soft and sentimental virtue, not a fuzzy feeling of romance. The love of which spiritual tradition speaks is "tough love," the connective tissue of reality—and we flee from it because we fear its claims on our lives. Curiosity and control create a knowledge that distances us from each other and the world, allowing us to use what we know as a plaything and to play the game by our own self-serving rules. But a knowledge that springs from love will implicate us in the web of life; it will wrap the knower and the known in compassion, in a bond of awesome responsibility as well as transforming joy; it will call us to involvement, mutuality, accountability.

"Love in action," said Dostoevski, "is a harsh and dreadful thing," and so it can be. A knowledge that springs from love may require us to change, even sacrifice, for the sake of what we know. It is easy to be curious and controlling. It is difficult to love. But if we want a knowledge that will rebind our broken world, we must reach for that deeper passion. We must recover from our spiritual tradition the models and methods of knowing as an act of love.

"Models and methods of knowing" may sound like an abstract topic, but it takes very concrete form in our daily lives. Those models and methods are institutionalized in the way we educate, in the formal and informal schooling to which all of us are exposed. The terrors of "the day after Trinity," my own defaults, and the distorted world-view of those students in the Carnegie Commission survey were created in part by the exploitative knowledge we teach and learn. How can the places where we learn to know become places where we also learn to love? How can we educate today so that "the day after" will be a time of compassion rather than combat? Some answers can be found, I believe, as we try to recover the spiritual ground of knowing, teaching, and learning.

A Prayerful Education

Any attempt to develop "a spirituality of education" is full of peril. It invites a host of resistances, distortions, and misunderstandings. Education is supposed to deal with the tangible realities of science and the marketplace. Spirituality is supposed to address an invisible world whose reality is dubious at best. Many of our schools are supported by the state which is legally barred from imposing religious claims on its citizens. The nurture of spiritual life is regarded as a function of family and church. So any effort to recover the spiritual grounds of education seems to run into that wall of separation we have erected between sacred and secular, private and public, the church and the state.

The challenge of this book—and its central irony—can be illustrated by the continuing debate over prayer in school. Many people yearn for a return of "religiousness" to education, so they press for laws permitting vocal prayer in the classroom. But I cannot join them. Vocal prayer in class dictates a consensus that does not exist in our pluralistic society, and any prayer that is so vaguely worded that it sounds agreeable to all is, by my limits, no prayer at all.

I cannot support such prayer because I am too deeply concerned about the problem it pretends to address. There is an illness in our culture; it arises from our rigid separation of the visible world from the powers that undergird and animate it. With that separation we diminish life, capping off its sources of healing, hope, and wholeness. We cannot settle for pious prayer as a preface to conventional education. Instead, we must allow the power of love to transform the very knowledge we teach, the very methods we use to teach and learn it.

While rejecting laws allowing moments of vocal prayer, I am

calling for a mode of knowing and educating that is prayerful through and through. What do I mean by prayer? I mean the practice of relatedness.

On one side, prayer is our capacity to enter into that vast community of life in which self and other, human and nonhuman, visible and invisible, are intricately intertwined. While my senses discriminate and my mind dissects, my prayer acknowledges and recreates the unity of life. In prayer, I no longer set myself apart from others and the world, manipulating them to suit my needs. Instead, I reach for relationship, allow myself to feel the tuggings of mutuality and accountability, take my place in community by knowing the transcendent center that connects it all.

On the other side, prayer means opening myself to the fact that as I reach for that connecting center, the center is reaching for me. As I move toward the heart of reality, reality is moving toward my heart. As I recollect the unity of life, life is recollecting me in my original wholeness. In prayer, I not only address the love at the core of all things; I listen as that love addresses me, calling me out of isolation and self-centeredness into community and compassion. In prayer, I begin to realize that I not only know but am known.

Here is the insight most central to spiritual experience: we are known in detail and depth by the love that created and sustains us, known as members of a community of creation that depends on us and on which we depend. This love knows our limits as well as our potential, our capacity for evil as well as good, the persistent self-centeredness with which we exploit the community for our own ends. Yet, as love, it does not seek to confine or manipulate us. Instead, it offers us the constant grace of self-knowledge and acceptance that can liberate us to live a larger love.

In prayer we allow ourselves to be known by love, to receive this freeing and redeeming knowledge of ourselves. In prayer we learn to know others and the world in the same loving way. The mind immersed in prayer no longer thinks in order to divide and conquer, to manipulate and control. Now, thinking becomes an act of love, a way of acknowledging our common bonds and assuming our rightful role in the created community.

Thomas Merton, who was also concerned with educating in love, once wrote that "the purpose of education is to show a person how to define himself authentically and spontaneously in relation to his world—not to impose a prefabricated definition of the world, still less an arbitrary definition of the individual himself."[6] Merton's words resonate with our secular, humanistic tradition, in which self and world are the great subjects of education and freedom and truth the great goals. But when education is not prayerful, when it does not center on transcendence, it fails to create authentic and spontaneous relations between the self and the world. Such an education allows self and world to imprison each other in prefabricated definitions that issue neither in freedom nor in truth.

When education divorces self and world from their transcendent source, they become locked in an endless power struggle to create each other in their own image. Since a self and a world that do not allow themselves to be known by love have a distorted self-image, the outcome of that struggle is always unfreedom and untruth. Such an education either turns out people who force their own inner distortions on the world, or it produces people who have succumbed to the world's distortion of themselves.

The self creates the world by means of projection. Much of the world's violence, for example, is an acting-out of the violence we find within ourselves, an effort to get rid of our inner demons by projecting them "out there." We help create the outward enemy (be it Russians or Asians, blacks or WASPs) to distract us from the inward enemy who always threatens to overcome us. More subtly, the self creates the world by forcing it into the limits of our own capacity to know. If we can know only what is available to our senses and our logic, then reality is reduced to those narrow terms.

The world creates the self by means of conditioning—the very systems of conditioning with which education is so preoccupied.

Taken as a physical-chemical system, the world shapes us into creatures governed by bodily needs and desires. Taken as a political system, the world casts us in the roles of exploiters or victims of power. Taken as a system of ideas, the world makes us into pure minds. And since education takes the world in all these ways and more, breaking it into fragments called "disciplines" with little attempt at unity, we finally understand ourselves as having no more coherence than the fragmented world itself.

Only by transcending self and world can we find the authenticity and spontaneity, the truth and freedom, of which Merton speaks. As long as we stay locked in their closed logic, allowing self and world to circle each other in an endless quest for power, we have little choice: dominate or be dominated. But when we know self and world from the vital center touched in prayer— and when our prayer allows us to be known—then we are free from the cycle of dominance, free to love the world, each other, and ourselves. An education in transcendence prepares us to see beyond appearances into the hidden realities of life—beyond facts into truth, beyond self-interest into compassion, beyond our flagging energies and nagging despairs into the love required to renew the community of creation.

We must resist the popular tendency to think of transcendence as an upward and outward escape from the realities of self and world. Instead, transcendence is a breaking-in, a breathing of the Spirit of love into the heart of our existence, a literal in-spiration that allows us to regard ourselves and our world with more trust and hope than ever before. To experience transcendence means to be removed—not from self and world, but from that hall of mirrors in which the two endlessly reflect and determine one another. Prayer takes us out—not out of self and world, but out of their closed, circular logic.

If our education, and our knowledge itself, became prayerful through and through, we would create a great countercurrent to the tides of cynicism and violence in this "well educated" society of ours. Formed in transcendence, the knowledge of physical science would be less readily translated into devices to destroy the

ecology of earth; the insights of social science would be less easily turned into programs of social and political manipulation that
break our faith with one another; and literary studies would be
less likely to breed cultured despisers of our common life. An
education in transcendence would open us to compassion and
the great work of co-creation.

Knowing Face to Face

I have spoken of spirituality in general terms so far, but now I
must become more specific. There is no such thing as "spirituality in general." Every spiritual search is and must be guided by a
particular literature, practice, and community of faith. In my definition of transcendence I have already suggested the source on
which this book draws. It is the Christian tradition, whose central
claim is not that God takes us out of ourselves and our world into
etheral realms, but that God broke in to reveal us and our world
as we are: "And the Word became flesh and dwelt among us, full
of grace and truth" (John 1:14). In this movement Spirit and
matter were fused and made whole; the distinction we make
between sacred and secular was overcome; self and world were
permeated with transcendent possibility, the possibility of love.

In Christian tradition, truth is not a concept that "works" but
an incarnation that lives. The "Word" our knowledge seeks is
not a verbal construct but a reality in history and the flesh. Christian tradition understands truth to be embodied in personal
terms, the terms of one who said, "I am the way, and the truth,
and the life." Where conventional education deals with abstract
and impersonal facts and theories, an education shaped by Christian spirituality draws us toward incarnate and personal truth. In
this education we come to know the world not simply as an
objectified system of empirical objects in logical connection with
each other, but as an organic body of personal relations and re-
sponses, a living and evolving community of creativity and compassion. Education of this sort means more than teaching the
facts and learning the reasons so we can manipulate life toward

our ends. It means being drawn into personal responsiveness and accountability to each other and the world of which we are a part.

The most lyrical expression of these themes is found in Paul's famous teaching on love in 1 Corinthians 13:

> If I have all the eloquence of men or of angels, but speak without love, I am simply a gong booming or a cymbal clashing. If I have the gift of prophecy, understanding all the mysteries there are, and knowing everything, and if I have faith in all its fullness, to move mountains, but without love, then I am nothing at all. . . .
>
> Love is always patient and kind; it is never jealous; love is never boastful or conceited; it is never rude or selfish; it does not take offense, and is not resentful. Love takes no pleasure in other people's sins but delights in the truth; it is always ready to excuse, to trust, to hope, and to endure whatever comes.
>
> Love does not come to an end. But if there are gifts of prophecy, the time will come when they must fail; or the gift of languages, it will not continue forever; and knowledge—for this too, the time will come when it must fail. For our knowledge is imperfect and our prophesying is imperfect; but once perfection comes, all imperfect things disappear. When I was a child, I used to talk like a child, and think like a child, and argue like a child, but now I am a man, all childish ways are put behind me. Now we are seeing a dim reflection in a mirror; but then we shall be seeing face to face. The knowledge that I have now is imperfect; but then I shall know as fully as I am known.
>
> In short, there are three things that last: faith, hope and love; and the greatest of these is love.

On this "day after Trinity," two thousand years after Paul's words were written, we can appreciate what Paul means when he says that our present knowledge is "imperfect," that "the time will come when it must fail." He describes the sources of that failure with unerring accuracy when he likens our knowledge to "a dim reflection in a mirror"—the reflections created by a self and a world endlessly looking for chances to shape and dominate each other, reflections that distort the world and ourselves.

But Paul goes beyond criticism to give us an image of the

knowledge we must seek: "then we shall be seeing face to face."
This is the personal knowledge toward which Christian spirituality calls us, a knowledge that does not distance us from the world
but brings us into community, face to face. A knowledge that
heals and makes whole will come as we look creation in the eyes
and allow it to look back, not only searching nature but allowing
it to search us as well. This will be perfect knowledge, Paul says,
for "then I shall know as fully as I am known." The "objects"
of our knowledge will no longer be objects but beings with personal faces, related to us in a community of being, calling us into
mutuality and accountability. It will be as the poet Rilke says,
". . . There is no place at all that isn't looking at you—you must
change your life."

Yet Paul understands that we are between the times, between
the dim knowledge that distorts our lives and the truth that sees
us whole. So Paul urges us to reach for the deepest source of
knowledge—love—allowing it to transform our way of knowing
and being. This love "is always patient and kind; it is never
jealous . . . never boastful or conceited." Transformed by love,
we do not arrogantly impose our powers on the world around us
or allow the world to overcome us. Transformed by love we use
our minds to recall and recreate the community in which we
were created, to know the world in the same spirit in which we
are known.

2. Education as Spiritual Formation

Monastic Disciplines and the School

In Genesis we are told that humankind was first formed "in the image of God," the image of love. But as we move from myth to human history, the image of God within us becomes dim or forgotten, distorted or obscured. From the moment of birth other powers imprint our souls with images less than divine.

Spiritual communities have long recognized how difficult it is to affirm the reality of love when history and our own biographies offer so much evidence of division, destruction, and death. So they have developed spiritual disciplines, daily practices by which we can resist these deformations of self and world, recalling and recovering that image of love which seems hidden or beyond reach. Through the disciplines of spiritual formation we seek to be re-formed in our original, created image.

These disciplines have been especially emphasized in the monastery, that ancient form of spiritual community in which our schools have one historic taproot, and from which we can recover a sense of education as a process of spiritual formation.[1] From monastic tradition I have learned three spiritual disciplines, three ways of maintaining contact with love's reality in the midst of misleading appearances: the study of sacred texts, the practice of prayer and contemplation, and the gathered life of the community itself.

Through the study of sacred texts, I maintain contact with the spiritual tradition, with the seeking and finding of those who have gone before. These texts allow me to return to times of deeper spiritual insight than my own, to recollect truths that my culture obscures, to have companions on the spiritual journey who, though long dead, may be more alive spiritually than many who are with me now. In such study my heart and mind are re-formed by the steady press of tradition against the distortions of my day.

I am also formed by prayer and contemplation, disciplines that take me beyond tradition into the living source of all spiritual life. In prayer and contemplation I seek immediate personal ex-perience of that to which tradition can only testify. If my tempta-tion in study is to be a mere observer of other people's spiritual lives, prayer and contemplation draw me into becoming a partici-pant, seeking a truth toward which others can point me but one I can finally only touch and taste for myself. If study forms me in images of love, prayer opens me to receive a love that is beyond imaging; it forms me in that receptiveness to love that is at the heart of the spiritual journey.

In the gathered life of the spiritual community, I am brought out of the solitude of study and prayer into the discipline of communion and relatedness. The community is a check against my personal distortions; it helps interpret the meaning of texts and gives guidance in my experience of prayer. But life in com-munity is also a continual testing and refining of the fruits of love in my life. Here, in relation to others, I can live out (or discover I am lacking) the peace and joy, the humility and servanthood by which spiritual growth is measured. The community is a disci-pline of mutual encouragement and mutual testing, keeping me both hopeful and honest about the love that seeks me, the love I seek to be.

These three spiritual disciplines sound far afield from what goes on in educational institutions. But our schools have not alto-gether lost their monastic imprint; they retain remnants of each of these practices. As we understand that fact, we begin to see how even secular eduction is a covert type of spiritual formation. My effort to develop a spirituality of education is not an imposi-tion of new and alien notions on the educational process. In-stead, it is an attempt to recall education to the forgotten roots and meanings of its routine practices.

The study of sacred texts has an obvious parallel in our schools. Students are formed by the reading they do, by the views of self and world such reading presents. Of course, the "sacred texts" of a secular society are not the ones held sacred in the spiritual tradition. But they are nevertheless held sacred in that society; between the lines, if not in the lines, they contain clues about our view of ultimate reality. The claims of physics, sociology, and analytic philosophy about ultimacy may be problematic from a spiritual viewpoint, but that is not my concern at the moment. I only wish to point out that these and kindred subjects are the "disciplines" to which our students are asked to "disciple" themselves. They contain the images of self and world in which our students are formed.

It is not so obvious that the disciplines of prayer and contemplation have their counterparts in secular education, but they do. The purpose of these disciplines is to see through and beyond the appearance of things, to penetrate the surface and touch that which lies beneath. In secular education this purpose is served by research and analysis, by various forms of empirical study and logical thought.

Education would not be necessary if things were as they seem. To go beyond appearances, education relies on fact and reason—on the capacity of science to dissect the world into its component parts, on the capacity of the mind to see the relation of these parts in rational orders. Prayer and analysis do not end up at the same point; where analysis aims at breaking the world into its elements, prayer aims at seeing beyond the elements into their underlying relatedness. But both prayer and analysis seek to make the world transparent. In this sense the school as well as the monastery engages in a contemplative discipline of formation.

Finally, educational institutions have a clear counterpart to the communal discipline of spiritual life. The whole culture of the academic community with its system of rewards and punishments works to shape our views of self and world. In fact, the rules and relationships of a school comprise a "hidden curriculum" which can have greater formative power over the lives of learners than the curriculum advertised in the catalogue. A business school may offer courses in team management and collective work styles, but if the culture of that school requires students to survive those courses through competition, then competition and not cooperation is the real lesson taught and learned. In a thousand ways, the relationships of the academic community form the hearts and minds of students, shaping their sense of self and their relation to the world.

Images of Knowledge

My formal education ended fifteen years ago, but I continue to reckon with the form it gave my life. Through the study of texts I mastered a body of knowledge that set my vocational course, shaping the way I would use my gifts and energies. By learning the skills of observation and analysis, I was given a certain freedom from conventions and appearances, thereby gaining independence of thought and action. Having survived the competition of the academic community, I formed a "successful" self-image that carried me confidently into adulthood (an adulthood that proceeded to batter my self-image, demanding a deeper source of assurance than success can ever provide).

But now I am aware that my education had an even deeper impact on my sense of self and world. "Impact" is not really the right word, for that suggests something sudden and forceful, something we cannot help but feel when it hits us. Instead, I mean a slow, subtle, nearly unconscious process of formation, something like the way a moving stream shapes the rocks over the long passage of time. The disciplines of textual study, observation and analysis, and community life are the channels through which that stream flows. What is the nature of the stream itself?

At its deepest reaches, education gave me an identity as a knower. It answered the question "Who am I?" by saying "You are one who knows." The knowledge I gained through education was more than a tool for my vocation; it became a source of my self-understanding as one whose nature it is to know. At the same time, eduction gave an identity to the world in which I live. In answer to the question "What is the world?" education said "The world is what your knowledge pictures it to be." The scope of the world became identical with the scope of my knowledge of it; my knowledge of the world became the world itself. And the same knowledge that gave me a picture of myself and the world also defined the relation of the two; that knowledge placed the world under my power. Education portrays the self as *knower*, the world as *known*, and mediates the *relation* of the two, giving the knowing self supremacy over the known world.

What is the nature of the knower? What is the nature of the known? And what is the nature of the relation between the two? These questions belong to a discipline called *epistemology*. It is an abstract and sometimes even esoteric inquiry into the dynamics of knowing. Its six-syllable name does not leap to our lips in normal conversation, and its insights appear remote from daily life. The several courses in epistemology that I took as a student seemed interminable and utterly irrelevant.

But now I understand that the patterns of epistemology can help us decipher the patterns of our lives. Its images of the knower, the known, and their relationship are formative in the way an educated person not only thinks but acts. The shape of our knowledge becomes the shape of our living; the relation of the knower to the known becomes the relation of the living self to the larger world. And how could it be otherwise? We have no self apart from our knowledge of the self, no world apart from our knowledge of the world. The way we interact with the world in knowing it becomes the way we interact with the world as we live in it. To put it in somewhat different terms, our epistemology is quietly transformed into our ethic. The images of self and world that are found at the heart of our knowledge will also be found in the values by which we live our lives.

I want to uncover some of those epistemological and ethical images by inspecting the key words we use to describe the kind of knowledge we value and trust—words like "fact" and "theory" and "reality" and "objective." Hidden inside our words, buried at their very roots, are ancient word-pictures which often tell us more than contemporary usage reveals. By digging to those roots and uncovering those images I hope to shed light on the epistemology that forms the educated self and its relation to the world.

The word "fact" is vital to us. Without it we would be virtually speechless if asked to describe the kind of knowledge we prize. Our commitment to "finding the facts" marks the turn from primitive superstition to modern science, from subjective knowledge based on feeling, intuition, and faith to objective knowledge that can be tested by our senses.

"Fact" comes from the Latin *facere*, "to make." The image of "making" suggests that a fact is something crafted by the human hand—a meaning most clearly seen in our words "manufacture" and "artifact." Here is something central to our sense of ourselves as knowers: we are busily engaged in trying to construct a liveable world with our facts.

It is no accident that our confidence in facts has grown as our religious faith has declined—the faith, I mean, that world has been created for us. We no longer see ourselves as recipients of the world as gift; we no longer regard knowing as a way of receiving and celebrating and using that gift. The knower now stands like a master builder in the midst of chaos, trying to fashion a world fit for human habitation. Now we alone are the creators; with our facts we make reality; the only reality we have is one made of those facts. We build a world by the sweat of what lies behind our brows, a task we pursue with pride in our power and success. But now it is pride and trembling, for in the midst of our labors we have sensed the precariousness of this mind-made world: when reality is what we make it, we can unmake it at any time.

Another key word is "theory." Our facts do not arrange themselves automatically into structures we can inhabit. So we spin theories, webs of connective logic, to order and integrate our facts. Theory is the thread that weaves our factual world together.

"Theory" comes from the Greek *theoros*, or "spectator," one of a complex of Greek words having to do with the sort of viewing and observing that characterize a theater audience. This image suggests another feature of modern knowing: we regard what we know as "out there," on stage, and we relate to it from a distance. Our knowledge does not draw us into relationship with the known, into participation in the drama. Instead, it holds us at arm's length as detached analysts, commentators, evaluators of each other and the world. Like theater-goers we are free to watch, applaud, hiss and boo, but we do not understand ourselves as an integral part of the action.

I realize that the Greeks regarded drama as integral to life, not a spectator sport but a soul-making force. But we, unlike the Greeks, make a rigid distinction between the observer and the observed for the sake of objectivity. Where Greek audiences were able to put themselves at the center of the play—literally allowing it to "play" upon them—we hold ourselves apart for fear of distorting the objective facts with our subjective needs.

"Objective" is another word central to our way of knowing. It is the ever present adjective, continually used to modify the key nouns so there will be no mistaking what we are talking about: objective facts, objectives theories, objective reality. If a claim is not objective, it is not knowledge but merely some species of passion or prejudice.

The Latin root of "objective" means "to put against, to oppose." In German its literal translation is "standing-over-againstness." This image uncovers another quality of modern knowledge: it puts us in an adversary relationship with each other and our world. We seek knowledge in order to resist chaos, to rearrange reality, or to alter the constructions others have made. We value knowledge that enables us to coerce the world into meeting our needs—no matter how much violence we must do. Thus our knowledge of the atom has brought us into opposition to the ecology of earth, to the welfare of society, to the survival of the human species itself. Objective knowledge has unwittingly fulfilled its root meaning: it has made us adversaries of ourselves.

Finally, the world "reality." Here is the standard by which we test all pretenders to the throne of knowledge. By modern standards myths and stories and poems, however entertaining they may be, have nothing to contribute to our knowledge since they are not about the "real" world. Neither does religion, of course, nor any other form of conviction or devotion. These are neither valid kinds of knowledge nor valid ways of knowing since they deal with something other than reality.

The root of "reality" is the Latin *res*, meaning a property, a possession, a thing—a meaning most clearly seen in our term "real estate." This image suggests another quality of modern knowledge: we seek to know reality in order to lay claim to things, to own and control them. No wonder poetry and religion are beyond the pale. Unlike physical and behavioral science, they do not give us title to any real estate. Perhaps we should rewrite the popular maxim "Knowledge is power" in language more to the point: "Real estate is power." Power comes from what we own and control, so the knowledge we value is that which gives us mastery over property. (Do we not speak of studying a subject in order to "master the field"?)

Of course, ownership and control are possible only in relation to objects or things. One cannot own a living being until, by a twist of mind, one turns it into a piece of property, a slave, thus gaining the dominance modern knowing strives for. Knowledge that gives us real estate must turn all its subjects—including nature and human beings—into objective things.

With these images of modern knowledge before us, we can return for a moment to the myth of Genesis. That story, which says that we were first formed in the image of love, also tells how that image was deformed by the action of Adam and Eve. God, who established Adam and Eve in Paradise, knew their human limits and so commanded them not to eat from the tree of knowledge of good and evil. They disobeyed. They reached for a knowledge that was beyond their limits, that would make them like God—and they were expelled from Paradise by the God who has no peer.

In the language of religious tradition, Adam and Eve committed the first sin. In the language of intellectual tradition, they made the first epistemological error. It was an error that has been repeated many times in human history, not least by those scientists of whom Robert Oppenheimer said, "The physicists have known sin."

The sin, the error, is not our hunger for knowledge—and the way back to Paradise is not via intentional ignorance (despite some latter-day Christian claims). Adam and Eve were driven from the Garden because of the *kind* of knowledge they reached for—a knowledge that distrusted and excluded God. Their drive to know arose not from love but from curiosity and control, from the desire to possess powers belonging to God alone. They failed to honor the fact that God knew them first, knew them in their limits as well as their potentials. In their refusal to know as they were known, they reached for a kind of knowledge that always leads to death.

From Objectivism to Truth

In the midst of this critique of modern knowing, it is important to recall how and why we came to value knowledge of this kind. The untrained mind of premodern times did not rely on factual observations and logical analysis but on the subjective faculties—emotion, intuition, faith. These modes of knowing do not manufacture a world to be held at arm's length, manipulated and owned. Instead, they receive the world as a given, an organic whole, and they make the knower an integral part of it. Such knowledge does not reduce the world to lifeless "things" but fills all things with vital, pulsing life. In such a world the very rocks have souls; flowers and trees have spirit-selves; the events of daily life are filled with symbols and signs. The whole of experience is pregnant with portent and meaning, and the knower is interwoven with it all.

This is the stuff of which fantasy is made—which doubtless explains why fantasy literature is so popular in our factual times.

But the premodern mentality, however attractive it may be to imaginations starved by scientism, has a sizable dark side. The frequent companions of emotion, intuition, and faith are superstition, crude ideology, and gross psychological projection. The teeming life of the earlier world was often little more than a reflection of the passions and prejudices of those who claimed to know.

We have no warrant to romanticize a time when witches were burned, heretics drawn and quartered, and farms and villages scorched to satisfy the psyches of princes, priests, and a frenzied populace. The commitment to objectivity has helped untangle some very twisted strands of the human soul, distortions we must stand "over against." Indeed, the commitment to objectivity has good spiritual grounding. It can be a hedge against the sin of self-centeredness which affects everything we do, including knowing, and has since Adam and Eve.

There is much about modern knowing we must honor. Its benefits are incontestable, not only in applied science but in the realm of culture as well. Our daily lives are lightened by the achievements of technology; the insights of social science have eliminated some of the cruelties of our common life; our spirits are freed to soar on the wings of literature and the arts. In this book I use the tools of modern knowing to criticize that knowing itself! Doing so is not an unconscious contradiction or a comic irony; it shows that modern knowing has the capacity to turn upon itself and open itself to correction, a capacity premodern knowledge did not possess. For all the dangers of modern knowing, we cannot go back.

But if the problem with primitive knowledge was the over-identification of the knower with the known, our problem is the estrangement and alienation of the two. In our quest to free knowledge from the tangles of subjectivity, we have broken the knower loose from the web of life itself. The modern divorce of the knower and the known has led to the collapse of community and accountability between the knowing self and the known world. This distortion is different in kind from that of the premodern world, but not in degree of danger. Indeed, it is more dangerous. We now have the power to magnify our distortion many times over, to destroy with our acts the community we have destroyed with our minds.

Having given some word-root images for this alienated mode of knowing, which I shall call objectivism, I want to offer a more systematic sketch of it. Objectivism begins by assuming a sharp distinction between the knower and the objects to be known. These objects exist "out there," apart from and independent of the knower. They wait, passive and inert, for us to know them. We, the knowers, are the active agents. We move into the field of objects equipped with tools that allow us to grasp them. Then we attempt to observe and dissect the objects by means of empirical measurement and logical analysis. At every step we are guided by procedural rules (e.g., the scientific method) guaranteeing that our knowledge will be objective—that is, that it will reflect the nature of the objects in question rather than the knower's whims. In order to assure the objectivity of what we know, we must report what we have discovered and how we discovered it so that others can confirm our findings. Truth, by this view, consists of propositions or reports that conform to the canons of evidence and reason, reports that can be reproduced by other knowers operating by the same rules.

Now, this sketch of modern knowing will be dismissed as a misleading caricature by readers familiar with certain trends in contemporary epistemology. They will rightly argue that my summary (while it may portray an early and naive stage of the struggle to escape from subjectivism) has been surpassed by theories of knowing that do not divorce the knower from the known, but that understand knowledge as a result of their dynamic interaction.

Some philosophers of science now argue that we can make no rigid distinction between the knower and the known, that every scientific finding is a mixture of "subjective" and "objective" elements. In atomic physics we now understand that the very process of measurement shapes our picture of the thing being measured, that the outcomes of any experiment are determined as much by the process of experimentation as by the nature of the object in question. As one philosopher writes:

> . . . The electron does not *have* properties independent of my mind. In atomic physics, the sharp Cartesian split between mind and matter, between I and the world, is no longer valid. We can never speak of nature without, at the same time, speaking about ourselves.[2]

And as another philosopher says:

> According to quantum mechanics there is no such thing as objectivity. We cannot eliminate ourselves from the picture. We are a part of nature, and when we study nature there is no way around the fact that nature is studying itself. . . . Scientists, using the "in here—out there" distinction, have discovered that the . . . distinction may not exist! What is "out there" apparently depends, in a rigorous mathematical sense as well as a philosophical one, upon what we decide "in here."[3]

The inseparability of the observer and the observed is even more obvious in the social sciences. In survey research or depth interviewing the answers people give are always influenced by subjective factors—the wording of the question, the tone of voice in which it is asked, the appearance of the interviewer, the expectations surrounding the topic. And in literary studies—despite recent efforts to study a novel "objectively" by counting adjectives and adverbs—we know that the reader brings personal experience to the writer's work to result in the outcome called "art."

The most searching exposé of objectivism has been made by Michael Polanyi.[4] He shows that both the individual scientist and the community of scientists are subjectively invested in every discovery of scientific fact. Polanyi demonstrates that the data of scientific experiments do not simply correlate themselves logically within a framework of abstract theory. They are correlated psychologically and even biologically within the person of the scientist, in a process that involves our bodies and our personal histories as well as our senses and rational minds. What we think of as abstract scientific reason really arises from, and remains rooted in, a personal "indwelling" of the scientist with the stuff of the physical world. And since the indwelling scientist has been shaped by membership in the scientific community, every finding of science is influenced by the relationships and commitments of this company of persons. For Polanyi, "knowledge is neither subjective nor objective but a transcendence of both achieved by the person."[5]

Given all these hedges, qualifications, and downright refutations of objectivism, what about my sketch of it? Is that sketch merely a caricature drawn for the sake of my argument? If not, how and where does it apply? The answer has been suggested by Richard Gelwick, one of Polanyi's leading interpreters:

> The separation of the knower and the known is no longer convincing *even though* that separation is *institutionalized* in our habits of thought, our ideals, and our organization of life.[6]

In particular, objectivism is institutionalized in our educational practices, in the ways we teach and learn. There, through the power of the "hidden curriculum," objectivism is conveyed to our students; our conventional methods of teaching form students in the objectivist world-view. If you want to understand our controlling conception of knowledge, do not ask for our best epistemological theories. Instead, observe the way we teach and look for the theory of knowledge implicit in those practices. That is the epistemology our students learn—no matter what our best contemporary theorists may have to say.

The teacher is a mediator between the knower and the known, between the learner and the subject to be learned. A teacher, not some theory, is the living link in the epistemological chain. The way a teacher plays the mediator role conveys both an epistemology and an ethic to the student, both an approach to knowing and an approach to living. I may teach the rhetoric of freedom, but if I teach it *ex cathedra*, asking my students to rely solely on the authority of "the facts" and demanding that they imitate authority on their papers and exams, I am teaching a slave ethic. I am forming students who know neither how to learn in freedom nor how to live freely, guided by an inner sense of truth.

If this is the case, then as a teacher I can no longer take the easy way out, insisting that I am only responsible for conveying the facts of sociology or theology or whatever the subject may be. Instead, I must take responsibility for my mediator role, for the way my mode of teaching exerts a slow but steady formulative pressure on my students' sense of self and world. I teach more than a body of knowledge or a set of skills. I teach a mode of relationship between the knower and the known, a way of being in the world. That way, reinforced in course after course, will remain with my students long after the facts have faded from their minds.

Of course, there are plenty of pedagogical experiments around these days, many proposals for innovative and engaging ways to teach and learn, but most of them deal only with techniques. They leave the underlying epistemology unexamined and unchanged; they are not well grounded in an alternative theory about the nature of knowing. Many of these experiments have failed, not only because the academy is wary of change, but because the experimenters have tried to change the form of teaching without altering its content. One does not develop a new pedagogy simply by choosing from a grab bag of teaching tricks. To find new ways of transmitting knowledge, we must first find a new knowledge. To find a better medium we must find a better message.

The message education should convey is not identified by words like "fact," "theory," "objective," and "reality" (though those words have their place). Instead, the message is called "truth." That word, once central to any discussion of knowing, teaching, and learning, was omitted from my earlier lexicon simply because it is not much used these days, not crucial to our conversations about the knowledge we value. Though people may still yearn for truth, it is widely felt in our disillusioned times that the word points either to a romantic illusion or an unreachable goal. To our skeptical ears, truth has a dreamy, airy, fantastic sound.

But when we examine the image hidden at the root of "truth" it turns out to be more immediate, grounded, and human than the words we know use to describe the knowledge we prize. The English word "truth" comes from a Germanic root that also gives rise to our word "troth," as in the ancient vow "I pledge thee my troth." With this word one person enters a covenant with another, a pledge to engage in a mutually accountable and transforming relationship, a relationship forged of trust and faith in the face of unknowable risks.

To know something or someone in truth is to enter troth with the known, to rejoin with new knowing what our minds have put asunder. To know in truth is to become betrothed, to engage the known with one's whole self, an engagement one enters with attentiveness, care, and good will. To know in truth is to allow one's self to be known as well, to be vulnerable to the challenges and changes any true relationship brings. To know in truth is to enter into the life of that which we know and to allow it to enter into ours. Truthful knowing weds the knower and the known; even in separation, the two become part of each other's life and fate.

So truth has nothing to do with manufacturing a world, keeping it at a distance, manipulating it to suit our needs, or owing it as property. Nor does it mean projecting our psyches on the world's screen. Rather, truth involves entering a relationship with someone or something genuinely other than us, but with whom we are intimately bound. Truth contains the image we are seeking—the image of community in which we were first created, the image of relatedness between knower and known that certain philosophies of science now affirm.

Educating toward truth does not mean turning away from facts and theories and objective realities. If we devote ourselves to truth, the facts will not necessarily change (though some may, since every fact is a function of relationship). What *will* change is our relation to the facts, or to the world that the facts make known. Truth requires the knower to become interdependent with the known. Both parties have their own integrity and otherness, and one party cannot be collapsed into the other. But truth demands acknowledgment of and response to the fact that the knower and the known are implicated in each other's lives.

In truthful knowing we neither infuse the world with our subjectivity (as premodern knowing did) nor hold it at arm's length, manipulating it to suit our needs (as is the modern style). In truthful knowing the knower becomes co-participant in a community of faithful relationships with other persons and creatures and things, with whatever our knowledge makes known. We find truth by pledging our troth, and knowing becomes a reunion of separated beings whose primary bond is not of logic but of love.

3. The Teaching Behind the Teaching

The Conventional Classroom

How is objectivism embedded in our conventional ways of teaching? What are the practices by which this theory of knowing and living are conveyed? After four years of college, two years of seminary, and five years of graduate study, it is not hard for me to describe the typical classroom practice—especially since I have taught this way myself more often than I care to recall!

With few exceptions, the classes I was in revolved around the activity and authority of one person—the teacher. My fellow students and I listened to the teacher's reports on reality or read the reports of other authorities whom the teacher chose and assigned. Our task was to memorize these reports so we could repeat them on exams. The highest level of personal involvement available to us in most classrooms was to ask the teacher questions about the lectures or the readings and to memorize the answers. Though some classes offered time for discussion, I seldom felt that I was being invited to teach the teacher, or even my fellow students—and seldom did I feel the impulse to try. The classroom was not a place for original inquiry but for imitation of authority, not a place of collaboration but of competition between learners.

I am not against lecturing, listening, and memorization. Done properly in the right context each of them has a role in creating the community of relatedness called truth. But in my educational experience, too much of the lecturing was authoritarian, too much of the listening was unengaged, too much of the memorization was mechanical—and the ethos of too many classrooms

was destructive of community. No matter what words are spoken
in such classrooms, the outcome of the method is to form students in objectivism's images of the knower and the known, the
self and the world. I want to suggest four ways in which this
happens, as well as four ways in which our teaching might
change if we took the new epistemologies, and truth itself, seri-
ously.

The Hidden Curriculum

First, in the conventional classroom the focus of study is always outward—on nature, on history, on someone else's vision
of reality. The reality inside the classroom, inside the teacher and
the students, is regarded as irrelevant; it is not recognized that *we*
are part of nature and of history, that we have visions of our
own. So we come to think of reality as "out there," apart from us,
and knowing becomes a kind of spectator sport. At best the classroom is a platform from which we view some subject.

I say the classroom is a platform "at best" because in many
classes students do not even get the chance to make their own
observations. Instead, they hear the reports of a teacher who
went out to explore reality and lived to tell the tale. Even more
likely, the teacher reports on the reports of other explorers, the
acknowledged authorities in the field. So the spectator-student is
often sitting in the far reaches of the upper grandstand, two or
three times removed from what is happening on the field.

It is no wonder that educated people (such as those students in
the Carnegie study) think of themselves as distant from the
world, uninvolved in its career. From our platform we observe
and analyze and assess, but we do not go into the arena—for that
is how we have been taught to know. This means that virtues
like compassion, the capacity to "feel with" another, are "educated away." In their place arises clinical detachment; counselors
and physicians are trained not to get involved with their clients,
journalists with their stories, lawyers with their cases. Involvement has its problems, but is detachment the solution? What

price do we pay for a journalism that reports murder and mayhem in the same voice as the opening of the Met? Or for medical training that ignores the healing potentials of the doctor-patient relationship?

If we believed that knowing requires a personal relation between the knower and the known (as some new epistemologies tell us) our students would be invited to learn by interacting with the world, not by viewing it from afar. The classroom would be regarded as an integral, interactive part of reality, not a place apart. The distinction between "out there" and "in here" would disappear; students would discover that we are in the world and the world is within us; that truth is not a statement about reality but a living relationship between ourselves and the world. But such an epistemology is rarely conveyed by our teaching; instead, objectivism is.

Second, because conventional education neglects the inner reality of teacher and students for the sake of a reality "out there," the heart of the knowing self is never held up for inspection, never given a chance to be known. The ideal of objectivism is the knower as a "blank slate," receiving the unadulterated imprint of whatever facts are floating around. The aim of objectivism is to eliminate all elements of subjectivity, all biases and preconceptions, so that our knowledge can become purely empirical. For the sake of objectivity, our inner realities are factored out of the knowledge equation.

This explains why the teacher is active and the students passive in the conventional classroom. The teacher is qualified to represent the facts because he or she has overcome subjective bias through long years of training. The students have not yet achieved this state of grace; they are still under the influence of emotions, prejudices, and whims. To invite students into active participation in knowing would be to risk the distortion of the facts by those passions. By keeping students passive and feeding them a steady diet of facts, we try to kill off their passions. Conventional education strives not to locate and understand the self in the world, but to get it out of the way.

On sober reflection, of course, this strategy makes little sense. What kind of world has no self in it, but only a "blank slate"? Such a world does not exist. What kind of self has no unique angle of vision, no special point of view? Such a self does not exist. And how can we believe that denying the students' passions will bring them under control? Ignored and suppressed, passion and prejudice tend to grow wild in one part of ourselves, while another more public part pretends to objectivity. This is exactly the condition of too many educated people today—they are capable of functioning with competence in a technological society, but they are possessed by the same inner darkness which engulfed Adam and Eve. As E. F. Schumacher writes:

> . . . World crises multiply and everybody deplores the shortage, or even total lack, of "wise" men or women, unselfish leaders, trustworthy counselors, etc. It is hardly rational to expect such high qualities from people who have never done any *inner work* and would not even understand what is meant by the words.[1]

If we believed that knowing is a process in which subjective and objective interact (as some new epistemologies tell us), we would create a different kind of education. Students and subject would meet in ways that allow our passions to be tempered by facts and the facts to be warmed up, made fit for human habitation, by passions. In this kind of education we would not merely know the world. We ourselves, our inner secrets, would become known; we would be brought into the community of mutual knowing called truth. But such an epistemology is rarely conveyed by our teaching; instead, objectivism is.

A third feature of the conventional classroom is its tendency to isolate the knowing self. The gathered group of students is not a true community, but a mere pedagogical convenience—the teacher can now report once to forty people rather than give the same report forty times. Objective knowledge involves a one-on-one encounter with the known; no other relationships are required. Even the so-called community of scholars consists largely of individuals checking up on the findings of other individuals.

In objectivism, there is no rationale for community, no impera-
tive for a mutual, interactive quest to know and be known.

In fact, objectivism, with its fear of subjective bias, is set
against community; if one person's prejudices are bad, how
much worse the multiplication of those prejudices in the ferment
of corporate life! So the conventional pedagogy is not only non-
communal but anticommunal. Students are made to compete
with one another as a hedge against error, so that only the fittest
and smartest will survive. If you think that I exaggerate the point,
remember that in many classrooms "cooperation" among students goes by the name of "cheating"!

It is no wonder that many educated people lack the capacity to
enter into and help create community in the world, that they
carry the habit of competition into all their relations with life. If
we believed that knowledge arises from the commitments of
communities (as some new epistemologies tell us) we would create classrooms where community was fostered, not feared. Our
students, having been formed in a knowing that springs from
communal commitments, would be better able to use their
knowledge to reweave community. But such an epistemology is
rarely conveyed by our teaching; instead, objectivism is.

The fourth effect of conventional educational education is simply the natural outcome of the three I have just explored: we
become manipulators of each other and the world rather than
mutually responsible participants and co-creators. We become
manipulators when we are schooled to be detached spectators of
a world "out there." Such distance helps make manipulation
possible. If our knowledge drew us close to the world in reverence and respect, if it made us realize that we are in the world
and the world is in us, we would not wish to manipulate the
world but to live in harmony with it and thus with ourselves.

We become manipulators when our knowledge leaves the inner self unexamined, for it is there that the drive for dominance
arises. If our knowledge made us aware of the heart of darkness
within, we would see our domineering instinct for the destructive
passion it is. Then we would wish not to subdue the world but to

have our own destructive impulses subdued by truth.

We become manipulators when education denies and destroys community, placing us in an endless competition for supremacy over each other. Throughout our education we learn to manipulate in order to survive, and then we carry that habit into our postgraduate lives. If we gained knowledge through a collaborative, communal process, we would possess a knowledge that could be used in cooperative, not manipulative, ways.

Some of the new epistemologies tell us that we can never speak of nature without, at the same time, speaking of ourselves. If we believed in this organic relationship of the knower and the known, we would create a classroom practice that would teach us not to rearrange the world but to learn its intricate relationships. The knower would become a person whose destiny is not to rule, but to raise to consciousness the interrelated quality of all of life, to enter into partnership with nature, history, society, and ourselves. But such an epistemology is rarely conveyed by our teaching; instead, objectivism is.

Many of us know what is wrong with the kind of teaching I have just described. The critics, and our own best instincts, have been telling us for years. But many of us continue to teach this way, and those who try to do it differently are too often defeated by seemingly insurmountable obstacles. How can we account for the persistence of a mode of teaching that has so many critics, so many obvious faults?

Some say that lecturing, assigning readings, and giving tests is simply the easiest way to teach, and that teachers (like everyone else) will take the line of least resistance. Others argue that mass education has forced this method upon us: how else do you teach a class of two hundred except with managerial techniques? Still others blame educational economics, pointing out that our underfunded schools are unable to buy the time or staff necessary for more personal and interactive modes of teaching and learning.

All of these explanations are factual and reasonable, but nothing in history would ever have changed if facts and reasons could not be overcome. Laziness, conceptions of efficiency, and bud-gets are not forced upon us by cosmic superpowers. They are all matters of choice, and we always have the freedom to choose otherwise. Why do we not choose otherwise? Why does this ped-agogy persist?

The critics have come closer to the answer by suggesting that this style of teaching persists because it gives teachers power. With power comes security: the security of controlling the class-room agenda, of avoiding serious challenges to one's authority, of evading the embarrassment of getting lost in territory where one does not know the way home. Teachers are unlikely to relin-quish such power even in the face of students who hunger for another way to learn.

But that is only half the story. Students themselves cling to the conventional pedagogy because it gives them security, too, a fact well known by teachers who have tried more participatory modes of teaching. When a teacher tries to share the power, to give students more responsibility for their own education, stu-dents get skittish and cynical. They complain that the teacher is not earning his or her pay, and they subvert the experiment by noncooperation. Many students prefer to have their learning boxed and tied, and when they are invited into a more creative role they flee in fear.

The conventional pedagogy persists because it conveys a view of reality that simplifies our lives. By this view, we and our world become objects to be lined up, counted, organized and owned, rather than a community of selves and spirits related to each other in a complex web of accountability called "truth." The con-ventional pedagogy pretends to give us mastery over the world, relieving us of the need for mutual vulnerability that the new epistemologies, and truth itself, imply.

Our persistent attraction to objectivist teaching and learning is the saga of Adam and Eve in history, not myth. We want a kind of knowledge that eliminates mystery and puts us in charge of an object-world. Above all, we want to avoid a knowledge that calls for our own conversion. We want to know in ways that allow us to convert the world—but we do not want to be known in ways that require us to change as well.

To learn is to face transformation. To learn the truth is to enter into relationships requiring us to respond as well as initiate, to give as well as take. If we became vulnerable to the communal claims of truth, conversion would be required. Our knowledge of the atom would call us to the patient work of peacemaking, not mindless acts of war; our knowledge of human nature would call us to the difficult task of cooperation, beyond our easy instinct to compete; our knowledge of nature would call us into careful nurturing, not careless exploitation, of the earth. But we find it safer to seek facts that keep us in power rather than truths that require us to submit. Objectivist education is a strategy for avoiding our own conversion. If we can keep reality "out there," we can avoid, for a while, the truth that lays the claim of community on our individual and collective lives.

Another Way to Teach and Learn

Several years ago I ran across an enigmatic tale about another kind of teaching and I have been meditating on it ever since. It comes from a collection of stories about the desert fathers and mothers, those fourth century seekers whose experience is so central to Christian tradition.[2] Since first reading that tale I have learned enough about these strange characters to realize why their radical experiment with truth is so important for our times.

First, they lived in an age when Christianity was emerging from four centuries of persecution into official recognition as the state religion of the Roman Empire. But these desert seekers were suspicious of any alliance between truth and power. Rather than take easy refuge in the official consensus, they left the great cities and went to the wastelands of Libya and Egypt to live there as hermits, to encounter truth on truth's own terms. We too must stand apart from the modern alliance of knowledge and power. We too must enter an uncharted space, beyond the familiar confines of the city of intellect, seeking another way to know and to teach.

Second, these hermits became the founders of the Western tradition of contemplative prayer. From their solitary quest came the monastic communities and, indirectly, the universities—both originally devoted to the kind of knowing humankind lost in the Fall, a knowing grounded in the love with which we are known.[3] If we want to recover the spirituality of education, to overcome the arrogance of the mind that would be God, we would do well to seek clues in the desert experience.

As the desert seekers went deeper into their dialogue with truth, they were often sought out as teachers. What they taught and how they taught it have come down to us in numerous anecdotes and tales. As we enter these stories with our hearts and minds, the desert teachers can become our teachers too. As we listen actively to their words, we will discover a conception of knowing and teaching quite different from the one that dominates education today. Hear, then, this story about Abba (Father) Felix and his students:

> Some brothers . . . went to see Abba Felix and they begged him to say a word to them. But the old man kept silence. After they had asked for a long time he said to them, "You wish to hear a word?" They said, "Yes, abba." Then the old man said to them, "There are no more words nowadays. When the brothers used to consult the old men and when they did what was said to them, God showed them how to speak. But now, since they ask without doing that which they hear, God has withdrawn the grace of the word from the old men and they do not find anything to say, since there are no longer any who carry their words out." Hearing this, the brothers groaned, saying, "Pray for us, abba."[4]

The students come to Abba Felix seeking a word. How does this teacher respond? He keeps silence—a long and painful silence. He does not answer with the quick verbal facility a teacher is supposed to have. He does not offer cheap and fluent grace. Instead, he takes a risk few teachers are willing to take—the risk of not speaking, of creating tension and embarrassment in a setting where they are supposed to fill the air with authoritative words. When Abba Felix finally does speak, he only intensifies the silence by saying "There are no more words nowadays."

Of course, there were plenty of words then, just as there are now, millions upon millions of them—the very words the hermits fled to the desert to escape. But they were not the words of truth, of relatedness with reality, the hermits sought. They were, and are, words of mastery, ownership, control, the kinds of words Abba Felix's students apparently wanted. They wanted words instead of life, reports instead of reality, words that would create the illusion of life while relieving them of responsibilty for living it, words of authority on which they could rely and retire.

So Abba Felix leads his students into a wordless world. He wants to humble their language, to break down the illusion that we can create reality with our words. He knows where our words and our world come from—that true words and the true world are not mental constructs but a gift of grace, a gift we can receive only as we abandon the illusion that our knowledge manufactures the world. Abba Felix takes his students deep into desert silence, a desolate space where none of their mind-made structures can survive.

Then Abba Felix tells them why the words of truth have disappeared. The words of truth have been taken from the teachers because their students did not follow them; truth has been withdrawn because the students failed to enter troth with what they learned. How does this teaching differ from the authoritarian, teacher-centered pedagogy I have been arguing with? In conventional education, it does not matter whether the students respond with their lives. The teaching does not make subjective claims on them; it is "objective." In conventional education, teacher, students, and subject are themselves autonomous objects, not related in a community of troth.

But in the desert, those relationships are central. There is a profound community of troth between Abba Felix, his students, and his words. If any one party breaks that troth, truth itself is broken. Abba Felix tells us that if truth is to be taught, then teaching and learning must take the shape of truth itself—a community of faithful relationships. Education in truth must bring teacher and students and subject into troth with each other, into the very image of the truth it hopes to convey.

The story tells us that it is not enough for students to record their teacher's words. It is not even enough for students to think about those words, weigh them, and give their mental assent. Learning the truth requires that we enter into personal relationship with what the words reveal. To know truth we must follow it with our lives. In this kind of education, the relationship between the teacher, the student, and the subject is one of obedience.

The word "obedience" does not mean slavish, uncritical adherence; it comes from the Latin root *audire*, which means "to listen." Obedience requires the discerning ear, the ear that listens for the reality of the situation, a listening that allows the hearer to respond to that reality, whatever it may be. Abba Felix himself is the example of authentic obedience. Confronted by students who disobey, who "ask without doing that which they hear," Abba Felix does not respond slavishly to his students' request for yet more empty words. Instead, he responds obediently to the reality of his students' lives; he faces the fact that they want words instead of life, and so he gives them silence instead of words. With this genuinely obedient response, Abba Felix uncovers the brokenness of their troth and leads his students to the threshold of new truth, new life.

The conception of truth as troth in this story is indicated by the fact that Abba Felix credits his students not only with the power to listen and respond to the teacher's words, but to *evoke* those words as well. Truth is evoked from the teacher by the obedience of those who listen and learn—and when that quality is lacking in students, the teacher's words are taken away. People who write about eduction often remind us that the root meaning of "to educate" is "to draw out" and that the teacher's task is not to fill the student with facts but to evoke the truth the student holds within. In the story of Abba Felix, the coin is turned. Here we see how students can draw out the teacher's truth, or silence and squelch it.

As a teacher I can find much comfort in this part of Abba

Felix's tale. It makes my students responsible for my lack of truthful words by their failure to follow truth with their lives. How beautifully the story echoes the doleful plaint of many college teachers, especially in the liberal arts: "How can I teach truth when my students are only interested in getting good grades that lead to good jobs and good money?" That complaint is not unreasonable, as every teacher knows who has felt the quickening of thought and feeling that comes when one has a student alive with a passion to learn. Students *do* evoke their teachers' words, and there is grim justice in the fact that mercenary students will draw mercenary teaching upon themselves.

But that is not the whole story. The teacher's plight cannot be passed off entirely on the students no matter how comforting for the teacher that might be. The story of Abba Felix, like every great story, has a subtle inner meaning. It is not only about the learner in the classroom but about the learner within the teacher. If we let our teacher-self speak without allowing our learner-self to listen and follow, our own truth, our troth with ourselves, will be broken. Such schizophrenia is an occupational hazard of teaching, the risk of becoming speakers of large and powerful words we fail to follow in the living. When that happens, we teachers lose our truthful words.

Taken that way, the story of Abba Felix helps me understand a painful period in my academic life. Schooled to speak and write, I used words in great volume for a number of years. Then came a time of dryness when I found it difficult to meet my classes, to speak in public, to write for publication or even for myself. That experience lasted for nearly two years. It made me desperate, angry, and despondent. I finally left my university career, convinced that conditions in the academy had caused my words to dry up.

But now I see the deeper lesson my experience was meant to teach. Words began to fail me because I was not following them with my life. I was failing to incarnate what truth I had been given, and my words, lacking flesh, were skeletons with no animation or powers of regeneration. Only as I began to act on the social concerns I had spoken about in class, only as I began trying to live the vision of community I had once written about, did my words begin to return.

My problem could also be put conversely. If I was failing to put my life where my mouth was, I was also failing to let my words emerge from the truth of my life. I was speaking about great possibilities without acknowledging how short my own life fell. Seldom do we live up to the truth we are given, but that does not mean we must cease speaking the truth. Instead, we must be obedient to the whole of our truth—including our frequent failure to live it out. If we can do that, with ourselves and with each other, the words of truth will continue to be given, and we will be given the power to live them more fully.

The story of Abba Felix begins with the students begging the teacher to "say a word," a word that remains lifeless in students who do not obey. But the story ends with the students asking for a word of another kind: " . . . the brothers groaned, saying, 'Pray for us, abba.'" It is important to understand what this petition means, for it shows that Abba Felix has led his students to the threshold of truth.

First, it reveals that the students have accepted responsibility for the demise of their teacher's words. They have acknowledged the brokenness of their troth with the teacher and his teaching. By asking for his prayer, they are asking for the reconciliation of community. Second, by asking for his prayer, the students reveal a deep understanding of the impasse their education has reached. Their problem is not technical but spiritual. It will not be resolved by better teaching and learning techniques, but only by their willingness to seek transforming knowledge. By asking for their teacher's prayer the students reveal their desire for conversion. Only through conversion can they enter into troth with themselves, their teacher, and the world. When " . . . the brothers groaned, saying, 'Pray for us, abba,'" it was not, as we might think, the forlorn ending to an unhappy story of failed education.

Instead, it shows that Abba Felix has led his students to the threshold of truthful knowing, the threshold of an education that is prayerful through and through.

Of course the story of Abba Felix comes from a distant time and place. It presupposes a culture of faith and learning quite different from our own. It might be dismissed as a relic—but that would be a mistake. For in its dynamics, the story has a timeless and universal quality. It reveals problems in education that are little changed today. It tells of students who are resistant to truth, of a teacher who is frustrated with them, of the breakdown of community in teaching and learning—it has a contemporary sound. But the story tells, too, of a teacher who knows how to respond, not merely with teaching techniques, but with a conception of truth grounded in a rigorous and demanding love. Abba Felix has much to teach us about teaching. But first we must learn more about the truth that animated his teaching, about the nature of the knowledge that enabled him to resist his students' pleas for more empty words. Only then will we be ready to explore ways of teaching and learning that might draw us toward obedience to truth in our own time.

4. What Is Truth?

Truth Is Personal

Christian faith in its original version, the version that guided
Abba Felix, is centered on a person who said, "I am . . . the
truth." Jesus did not say "I will speak true words to you" or "I
will tell you about the truth"; he claimed to embody truth in his
person. To those who wished to know truth, Jesus did not offer
propositions to be tested by logic or data to be tested in the
laboratory. He offered himself and his life. Those who sought
truth were invited into relationship with him, and through him
with the whole community of the human and nonhuman world.
Abba Felix's teaching, which centers on an invitation into personal relationship with reality, is faithful to the way Jesus taught.

Because primitive Christianity revolves around personal, not
propositional, truth, its richest insights come down to us in stories about people. Here is one such story. In it we witness a
challenge to the kingdom of objectivism. Through it we see an
alternate vision of truth and how truth is to be known.

The story comes from the eighteenth chapter of the Gospel
According to John. Jesus is brought before Pilate to be tried. Pilate asks Jesus if he is the king of his people. Jesus answers, "Do
you say this of your own accord, or did others say it to you about
me?" Pilate angrily responds that *he* is not one of Jesus' people,
that *they* have handed Jesus over to be tried, and demands that
Jesus explain why, asking, "What have you done?" Jesus replies,
"My kingship is not of this world," and as proof he reminds
Pilate that his followers did not fight the authorities to resist his
arrest and trial. Pilate, trying desperately to make worldly sense
of this unworldy argument, cries, "So you are a king?" Jesus
replies, "You say that I am a king. For this I was born, and for

this I have come into the world, to bear witness to the truth. Everyone who is of the truth hears my voice." And Pilate asks Jesus the famous question, "What is truth?"

Pilate's final question can be asked either with a cynical sneer or a despairing sigh, perhaps with a bit of both. But the cynicism and despair are not found in the word "truth," which we, with Pilate, so often utter only to suggest the unattainable or even the illusory. The bias is in that little word "what." With it, Pilate reveals himself to be the model objectivist. He is obsessed with the "whatness" of truth, while before him stands a person who claims to embody the truth—not an object "out there" but a subject who would enter into Pilate's own subject-life.

From the outset of their encounter Pilate tries to objectify Jesus by forcing him into the category of "king." He is trying to make Jesus a comprehensible and dispensable entity in the political terms of the time. But Jesus, the person, resists Pilate's categories. He asks, "Do you say this of your own accord, or did others say it to you about me?" suggesting that Pilate's opening question comes from impersonal caricature, not personal understanding. He says that his "kingdom" is not of this world, that it cannot be comprehended in objective political terms. He puts forward a personal claim related to his very birth about his reason for being. But Pilate is incapable of knowing this personal truth because he holds the person at arm's length, treating him as an object, a thing, a "what." By reducing truth to objective terms Pilate puts himself beyond truth's reach. Eventually, he assents to murdering a personal truth that calls for conversion in favor of an objectivism that leaves him in control.

The story suggests that in Christian understanding truth is neither an object "out there" nor a proposition about such objects. Instead, truth is personal, and all truth is known in personal relationships. Jesus is a paradigm, a model of this personal truth. In him, truth, once understood as abstract, principled, propositional, suddenly takes on a human face and a human frame. In Jesus, the disembodied "word" takes flesh and walks among us. Jesus calls us to truth, but not in the form of creeds or theologies or world-views. His call to truth is a call to community—with him, with each other, with creation and its Creator. If what we know is an abstract, impersonal, apart from us, it cannot be truth, for truth involves a vulnerable, faithful, and risk-filled interpenetration of the knower and the known. Jesus calls Pilate out from behind his objectivism into a living relationship of truth. Pilate, taking refuge behind the impersonal objectivist "what," is unable to respond.

The point I am making about Jesus as a paradigm of personal truth has often been distorted, sometimes by persons outside Christian tradition but most damagingly by persons within. Christians have too often spoken of "knowing Jesus" in a way that tends toward one of two extremes. Either the believer "knows" Jesus in a way that excuses him or her from knowing anything else (like physics or psychology or English literature), or the believer contains the "knowledge" of Jesus in a compartment labeled "religious" and engages in other forms of knowing as if there were no connection. When Christians "know" Jesus in these ways, it is right and proper for others to reject their "truth" as either irrelevant to the rest of life or productive of the sort of principled ignorance that has bred so much evil.

When Jesus said, "I am . . . the truth," he was not making an idiosyncratic claim about a private individual, not inviting us into an isolated relationship that is either the whole of what we must know or separable from all the rest. He claimed neither that his mind contained all truths nor that his truth freed us from the need to seek truth in its manifold forms. Instead, he was announcing and incarnating a new understanding of reality and our relation to it. Truth—wherever it may be found and in whatever form—is personal, to be known in personal relationships. The search for the word of truth becomes the quest for community with each other and all creation. The speaking of that word becomes the living of our lives.

As we enter this relationship called truth, we discover not only a person called Jesus, not only the truth in ourselves and other persons, but an entire universe which, in the words of Martin

Buber, is no longer only "It" but thoroughly and profoundly "Thou." The word of truth that Jesus made personal is the Word through whom "all things were made" and without whom "was not anything made that was made" (John 1:3). We are to learn and live in bonds of Thouness, of community, not only with other people but with all the nonhuman forms of life the universe contains. For Christians to understand anything less from Jesus' witness is to objectify and diminish Jesus, to limit God's truth, to fail a world that needs desperately to be addressed as "Thou."

I realize that this interpretation of the personal truth of Jesus will not, at first glance, put non-Christians at ease. They will suspect me of trying to Christianize the universe, of wanting to put the whole of creation under a theological umbrella that leaves other spritualities out in the rain. Such people may understandably wish that I would put Jesus back in the box and keep my faith irrelevant.

But by my view the personal truth of Jesus in not divisive and discriminatory. It is ultimately capacious. As Paul says, life in Christ breaks down all the cultural distinctions between us (Gal. 3:28). I am not arguing for an objectivist theology that aims at pushing or pulling all persons into doctrinal comformity or church membership. It is not necessary to accept Jesus as Lord and Savior in order to find in him a paradigm of personal truth. To say that truth is personal is to affirm the image of truth that lies within each person, regardless of creed or institutional affiliation. Indeed, if truth is personal, then creeds and institutions are only the objectified shells of the truth-seeking life that pulses in every human heart. We will find truth not in the fine points of our theologies or in our organizational allegiances but in the quality of our relationships—with each other and with the whole created world. A Martin Buber who understands the Thouness of reality embodies personal truth in his Jewishness more deeply than some Christians seem able to do.

These issues of interreligious understanding are important. But it is even more important to recognize that narrow-minded or triumphalistic spiritualities are not the major obstacle to a universal community of nature and humankind. The major obstacle is an objectivism that persists in making "things" of us all. This objectivism—with only a little prompting from religious or secular ideologies—is quickly translated into political and social programs of division, manipulation, and oppression. The threat to community posed today by certain sectarian movements (whether the Christian Moral Majority or the Islamic fundamentalists) comes not from the heart of their spiritual traditions but from an objectivism that reduces everyone not in their fold to mere objects for conversion if possible, or elimination if necessary. The personal truth embodied in Jesus stands against all such distortions, not the least those committed in his name.

Our Capacity for Relationship

The personal truth of Christianity, with its emphasis on the quality of our relationships, is usually understood as an ethic, an approach to living—not as an epistemology, an approach to knowing. I have shown how the objectivist epistemology becomes an ethic of detachment and manipulation. Now I want to show how the ethic of Christian personalism becomes an epistemology of participation and accountability. As I do so, I hope also to show how some of our contemporary theories of where knowledge comes from simply confirm this ancient and "primitive" way of knowing.

The first question any epistemology must answer has been posed by E. F. Schumacher: "What enables a man to know anything at all about the world around him?"[1] That question and the first step toward an answer come down to us from ancient tradition, as Schumacher suggests:

> "Knowing demands the organ to be fitted to the object," said Plotinus. . . . Nothing can be known without there being an appropriate "instrument" in the makeup of the knower. This is the Great Truth of *adaequatio* . . . the understanding of the knower must be *adequate* to the thing to be known. . . . "Knowledge [said

Thomas Aquinas] comes about insofar as the object known is
within the knower."[2]

The theory of *adaequatio* is obviously sound. The knower must
have some inner capacity to receive the known if knowledge is to
result from their encounter. If we lack the capacity to imagine a
fourth dimension, we will never know anything more than a
three-dimensional world. But what are the capacities or instruments that enable us to know the world? Objectivism answers:
our sense organs, which can apprehend objects, and our minds,
which can relate those objects in rational, logical patterns. By this
view, knowledge emerges as these capacities for knowing inter-
cept a reality whose essential structure is empirical and logical.

But why assume that sensation and rationality are the only
points of correspondence between the human self and the world?
Why assume so, when the human self is rich with other capacities—intuition, empathy, emotion, and faith, to name but a few?
If there is nothing to be known by these faculties, why do we
have them? Are they merely for our amusement in the midst of
an unamusing universe that can be known by sensation and reason alone? Or are these nonempirical, nonrational faculties of
ours one side of an *adaequatio*, the other side of which is a world
whose wholeness can be known only as these faculties are
brought into full partnership with our senses and reason? We
ourselves are part of the reality we wish to know: does the multiplicity of our modes of knowing suggest a similar multiplicity in
the nature of that reality?

The Christian understanding of *adaequatio* goes beyond sensation and rationality to the reality of the whole person. The first
step in that direction has been taken by Schumacher himself:

> The answer to the question "What are man's instruments by
> which he knows the world outside him?" is ... quite inescap-
> ably this: "Everything he has got"—his living body, his mind,
> his self-aware Spirit. ... It may even be misleading to say that
> man has many instruments of cognition, since, in fact, the *whole
> man* is one instrument. ... The Great Truth of *adaequatio* teaches

us that restriction in the use of instruments of cognition has the inevitable effect of narrowing and impoverishing reality.[3]

When we consider the whole person we find more than sense and reason, more than a collection of instruments of cognition, more even than the "one instrument" Schumacher rightly claims the person is. We find all of this, but ultimately we find a self whose nature is not simply to know, but to know in relationship, as a means to relationship. The self is greater than the sum of its parts, and its greatness is in its ability to move beyond perception in any mode—beyond the isolation of the observer—into relationship with the world to be known. The self is above all communal, and its communality draws on "everything we have got."

The relationships of the self require not only sensory evidence of the other; not only logical linkages of cause and effect; they also require inner understanding of the other, which comes from empathy; a sense of the other's value, which comes from love; a feel for its origins and ends, which comes from faith; and a respect for its integrity and selfhood, which comes from respecting our own. The most expansive *adaequatio* between ourselves and the world—one that does not narrow and impoverish reality—is found in our capacity for relationship. In relating to the other we find ourselves drawing on "instruments" the observer role never evokes. As our relatedness is called out, we find ourselves knowing reality more deeply and roundly than the observer ever can.

The structure of reality is not exhausted by the principles of empiricism and rationality. Reality's ultimate structure is that of an organic, interrelated, mutually responsive community of being. Relationships—not facts and reasons—are the key to reality; as we enter those relationships, knowledge of reality is unlocked. Human beings are not the only participants in that community, but we alone are capable of participating in self-aware and articulate ways. As our capacity for conscious and reflective relationship increases, so does our knowledge. The deepest calling in our quest for knowledge is not to observe and analyze and alter things. Instead, it is personal participation in the organic community of human and nonhuman being, participation in the network of caring and accountability called truth.

The crucial difference between observing and relating is that a relationship is always two-way. As we use the full range of human instruments to know reality, we find that we are also known. The world we can know through our senses and our logic is a world that cannot speak back to us, speak to us about ourselves. With this limited mode of knowing, not only does the nonhuman world remain inarticulate, but the human world is deprived of *its* voice as we transform people into objects, things. But when we know through our other capacities as well—empathy, intuition, compassion, faith—we pick up the world's subtle signals, its subvocal speech, its messages to us about our limitations and responsibilties and potentials. When we allow the whole self to know in relationship, we come into a community of mutual knowing in which we will be transformed even as we transform.

The truest passion behind our need to know is the desire to reweave that community and take our proper place in it. To search for truth is to reach out with our whole persons for relationships which can re-form us and the world in the original image of love. To know the truth is to enter with our whole persons into relations of mutuality with the entire creation—relations in which we not only know, but allow ourselves to be known.

Truth Is Communal

The claim that truth is personal must be defined and qualified with care, for the major movement against objectivism today—against the tyranny that makes us and our world into "things"—is a form of knowing that reduces personal truth to private terms. In our resistance to objectivism, we tend toward an equally dangerous subjectivism. Once we have seen that reality is not "out there," we too easily settle for a reality "in here," for a truth that consists of little more than our private perceptions and needs.

"One truth for you, another for me, and never mind the difference" is the simplistic slogan of many who flee from the objectivist tyranny.

Ironically, this effort to liberate the world from objectivism ends up by imprisoning the world once more. If my private perceptions are the measure of truth, if my truth cannot be challenged or enlarged by the perceptions of another, I have merely found one more way to objectify and hold the other at arm's length, to avoid again the challenge of personal transformation. This view isolates the self, creates as many worlds as there are knowers, destroys the possibility of community, and finally makes the other an object of no real account. Whether I look upon your world with envy or disgust, it can never be my world. You and your reality are only objects to be viewed, not relationships to be entered. The impulse behind subjectivism may be anti-objectivist, but it takes us to the same end, a place where truth has no chance to weave us and our world together in a community of accountability and mutual change.

The subjectivist theory of knowing, like its objectivist counterpart, finds expression in teaching. There are some classrooms where the private self reigns, where truth is reduced to what that self sees and feels and wants. Such a pedagogy not only neutralizes other selves; it has the same effect on the subjects we study. If the criteria of truth are my perceptions and my needs, what claim can the study of science or history or literature make on my life? This way of teaching and learning is simply one more strategy for avoiding transformation. If private knowledge (no matter how full and rich) is the measure of all things, I can never be drawn into encounter with realities outside myself—especially those that might chastize and correct me. When truth is merely "in here" we lose touch with truth's transcendence, with the critique of our illusions that comes from participating in a community of troth.

By Christian understanding, truth is neither "out there" nor "in here," but both. Truth is between us, in relationship, to be found in the dialogue of knowers and knowns who are understood as independent but accountable selves. This dialogue saves personal truth from subjectivism, for genuine dialogue is possible only as I acknowledge an integrity in the other that cannot be reduced to my perceptions and needs. To say that truth is personal is not to confine truth to private, subjective terms. To encounter the other as a person is to encounter the most objective, irreducible reality in the universe—a *person*, who, unlike a thing, actively resists our most determined efforts to diminish him or her to our limited, self-serving images.

The radical objectivity of the person is illustrated in the encounter of Jesus and Pilate. Pilate tries to force Jesus into the political categories of the time, saying, "You *are* a king, then?" But Jesus, the person, resists. He refuses to be reduced to Pilate's terms; he asserts his own integrity and personhood. He says, "'King' is *your* word"—and proceeds to tell Pilate how he understands himself.

Here is an important paradox. Objectivism, by reducing the world to a collection of things, places the knower in a field of mute and inert objects that passively succumb to his or her definitions of them. In this sense, objectivism creates the most subjective of worlds, a world created in our own images, a world of objects that cannot fight back and assert their own selfhood. But when we try to know the world in terms of personal truth— relating to each other, to history, to nature, as selves in conversation—then we everywhere meet the person, who refuses to succumb to our private distortions of reality.

Personal truth gives voice to dumb creatures and mute objects—as well as to those humans whom our science has silenced. It allows them to speak their truth to knowers who want to listen obediently, knowers whose aim is not manipulation and mastery but membership in the community of truth. The apparent subjectivism of the claim "truth is personal" creates a world in which we experience the other's independence from our whims, a world of more externality and accountability than that created by objectivism itself.

Does it seem that I am stretching a point when I claim that

personal truth leads not toward individualism but toward a community of relationship, dialogue, and mutual transformation? If so, it is only because objectivism has taught us to regard "the person" as one more isolated object among others. We forget that a person can be a person only in community. Whether we are aware of it or not, each of us is a community in microcosm. The personhood of each of us is shaped by a moving inward intersection of numerous selves—family and friends and colleagues and strangers. If we are to grow as persons and expand our knowledge of the world, we must consciously participate in the emerging community of our lives, in the claims made upon us by others as well as our claims upon them. Only in community does the person appear in the first place, and only in community can the person continue to become.

This community consists of more than other human selves. We are also in community with the material world, with plants and animals, with God. Our human nature links us up and down that "great chain of being," with the divine in whose image we were created and with the earth through which that creation arose. We are but one link in that chain and our knowing must take account of all the other links. To live in ignorance or disdain of any of these connections is to put our own lives, and all other life, at peril—as the objectivist way of knowing has done.

The Mutuality of Truth

In personal knowing, the relation of the knower and the known does not conform to the stiff protocol of observer and observed. It is more like the resonance of two persons. When we know something truly and well, that which we know does not feel like a separate object to be manipulated and mastered. Instead, we feel inwardly related to it; knowing it means that we have somehow entered into its life, and it into ours. Such knowledge is a relationship of personal care and fidelity, grounded in troth. In the words of Abraham Joshua Heschel (another Jew who, like Buber, has a profound understanding of personal truth), "It is impossible to find Truth without being in love."[4] In the words of St. Gregory, "Love itself is knowledge; the more one loves the more one knows."[5]

This intimate link between loving and knowing is implicit throughout the Judeo-Christian Scriptures. The Hebrew Bible uses the word "know" to indicate the conjugal relation of husband and wife (as in "Abraham knew Sarah"), the same word it uses for our knowledge of God and of the created world. The most common New Testament word for "know" is also used for lovemaking. The images that inform the biblical understanding of what it means to know—images of personal involvement and mutuality—are neither accidental nor antiquated. They reflect the quality of knowing at its deepest reaches, the quality of a truth that draws us into community.

Earlier I noted that some philosophers of science now argue that all knowledge involves a personal investment of the knower in the known. Michael Polanyi shows that even in the "hardest" of the "hard" sciences the knower brings personal elements to every act of knowing—if only his or her commitment to be concerned about *this* phenomenon rather than *that*. For Polanyi, too, knowing proceeds by a kind of love:

> I have shown that into every act of knowing there enters a passionate contribution of the person knowing what is being known, and that this coefficient is no mere imperfection but a vital component of his knowledge.[6]

Polanyi's insights are obviously allied to the view that truth is personal. But by Christian understanding we must go one step further—and it is a critical step. Not only do I invest my own personhood in truth and the quest for truth, but truth invests itself personally in me and the quest for me. "Truth is personal" means not only that the knower's person becomes part of the equation, but that the personhood of the known enters the relation as well. The known seeks to know me even as I seek to know it; such is the logic of love.

When academics speak of "the pursuit of truth," they rightly imply that a gap exists between ourselves and truth. But there is a conceit hidden in that image, the conceit that we can close the gap as we track truth down. In Christian understanding, the gap exists not so much because truth is hidden and evasive but because we are. We hide from the transforming power of truth; we evade truth's quest for us. That is why Abba Felix and his fellow seekers went into the desert, into solitude and science: they were trying to sit still long enough, in a space open enough, that truth could find them out, track them down. The truth that sought them was not an inert object or proposition. Rather it had the active quality of a person who wished to draw them into a community of mutual knowledge, accountability, and care.

By this understanding, I not only pursue truth but truth pursues me. I not only grasp truth but truth grasps me. I not only know truth but truth knows me. Ultimately, I do not master truth but truth masters me. Here, the one-way movement of objectivism, in which the active knower tracks down the inert object of knowledge, becomes the two-way movement of persons in search of each other. Here, we know even as we are known.

To speak this way about knowing is not "merely poetic" (as if poetry could ever be mere!). Images such as these are faithful to our moments of deep knowing. Many of us, for example, have had the experience of reading a great novel and suddenly becoming aware that it is reading us as well. That is the mark of its greatness. The writer has created a living world with words, a vital communion that cannot be taken merely as an object of study but one that draws out our meanings even as we draw its meaning out.

One requisite of great writing is the ability to make a character come alive. By that we mean a capacity to go beyond the artful manipulation of words into the creation of a person who transcends the printed page. Who can claim that Melville's Captain Ahab or Dostoevski's Zossima are not in some intelligible sense "real persons," perhaps more real to us than some of the people in our daily lives? Such characters come off the page to converse with the reader; they seem to know us and our secrets at least as well as we know them; they reveal us to ourselves in ways not possible through simple self-analysis. Characters such as these are not mere projections of our psychological needs; they are independent selves capable of entering relationships. As Jung once said, "It is not Goethe who creates *Faust*, but *Faust* which creates Goethe." We discover the autonomy of such characters when they tell us things about ourselves we would rather not hear!

We may bring truth to light by finding it and speaking its name—but truth also brings us to life by finding and naming us. As we allow ourselves to be known by that which we know, our capacity for knowledge grows broader and deeper. The knower who advances most rapidly toward the heart of truth is one who not only asks "What is out there?" in each encounter with the world, but one who also asks "What does this encounter reveal about me?" Only as we allow ourselves to be known—and thus cleansed of the prejudices and self-interests that distort the community of truth—can we begin truly to know. When we allow ourselves to be known in truth, we are able to see and hear and feel more of the world's reality than we could before we were known.

Knowing All Things

The personal truth revealed in Jesus is not limited to knowledge of God alone. To allow such a limitation is to succumb to one of secularism's self-protective devices—the claim that this mode of knowing may apply to our spiritual lives but has nothing to do with the secular knowledge on which modern life depends. To allow such a limitation is to make God one more object among others and to violate the premise of faith that *all things* were made by God's personal Word.

How does personal truth apply to other kinds of knowledge? It seems easy enough to extend it to the study of literature whose characters can, in some sense, enter a dialogue with us. But what about philosophy, the study of abstract ideas? What about history and the social sciences, whose subjects are either dead or statistical? And what about natural and physical science, whose subjects are mute or inert? Do I really mean to suggest that rocks and trees and stars can speak to us as persons?

"Personhood" and "community" are clearly metaphors when applied to the sociologist's data, the geologist's rock strata, or the objects of the astronomer's gaze. These are not persons in the immediate sense that you and I are, nor are we in community with them in the exact sense that we are in community with other human beings. But every kind of knowing proceeds by metaphor. Objectivism uses the metaphor of "objects" for persons and communities that do not conform to the literal meaning of that term. If objectivist social science can make "things" out of people and their lives, we can apply the metaphor of "person" to the nonhuman and nonliving things of the world. The purpose of metaphor is to open our understanding to new possibilities. What possibilities are opened for us by the metaphors of personal truth?

In the study of history and social science, those possibilities seem clear and compelling. By entering into community with the past and with the lives represented by the sociologist's statistics, we are simply reclaiming a truth that objectivism ignores: the community to which we belong extends far beyond the persons with whom we live daily; it extends backward into time and outward into the larger world. To approach such studies in any other way is to diminish our knowledge, not only of history and society but of ourselves.

A striking example of personal truth in the study of history is found in the work of Louis Massignon, the twentieth-century scholar whose research made the West aware of al-Hallaj, ninth-century Muslim martyr and saint:

> By extraordinary affinity and sensitivity Massignon, a Christian, was able to cross over into historical, linguistic, religious and cultural consciousness of the other. He entered a profound friendship [with the] Muslim whose "passion" he was to transmit in a series of major studies. . . . Massignon himself always

> felt that he had been discovered and plumbed by Hallaj and that
> their linking was not a matter of investigative research or trans-
> cultural curiosity, but was a friendship, a love, a rescue.[7]

Here is a key characteristic of scholarship in the personal
mode, the sense that we have been "discovered and plumbed"
by the subject of the research itself, that truth is alive and active
in the subject, seeking us out even as we seek it.

Such a sense need not be limited to biographical research. It
can also emerge in the study of broader patterns, of historical,
anthropological, and sociological data. When students, for example, are taught the history of the Third Reich as a distant series of
objective events, they learn only half the truth—and since truth
is a relationship, they finally learn no truth at all. But when those
events are studied in ways that study the students themselves,
then the whole truth comes clear: the potential for such evil is in
every person and society, and this far-off history is really the
story of our own lives. When students are taught about primitive
peoples in ways that fail to reveal the grace that infuses those
lives and the "primitive" dimensions of our own, both we and
our subjects emerge less than fully known. For an alternative,
read Margaret Mead on the people of Manus.[8] And in sociology,
the possibility for mutual knowing between students and their
subjects seems self-evident. The interview, that favorite tool of
social data gatherers, is meant to be an "inter-view," a way of
looking into other people's behaviors and attitudes that opens
our own lives to view.

Personal truth applies to the study of nature and inanimate
objects as well. Do I mean that earth and rocks and trees and
animals are persons themselves, capable of speaking to us? Of
course not—when we approach them with our senses and logic
alone. Then they are only things. But when we approach them in
awareness of ourselves as whole persons who are communally
implicated with soil and squirrels and such, then we are able to
know these nonhuman beings as co-participants in the community of truth. By relating to them in the fullness of our own per-

sonhood we allow them in all their muteness to speak to us as persons, to "discover and plumb" us in a knowing that makes us accountable to their interests and needs.

Read Loren Eiseley, for example, to sense the potential for re-searching nature in ways that allow us to be re-searched as well. When Eiseley ruminates on the fossil remnants of long-dead beasts, the dialogical quality of his knowing allows us to discover the animal and the prehistoric lurking in our own backbones.[9] Or read Aldo Leopold as he makes the case for an ethic of the earth:

> All ethics so far evolved rest on a single premise: that the indi-vidual is a member of a community of interdependent parts. . . .
> The land ethic simply enlarges the boundaries of the community to include soils, waters, plants, and animals, or collectively: the land. . . . In short, a land ethic changes the role of *Homo sapiens* from the conquerer of the land-community to plain member and citizen of it. It implies respect for his fellow-members, and also respect for the community as such.[10]

An ecological ethic depends on an ecological epistemology, a way of knowing the physical world that approaches its nonhu-man members as coparticipants in the community of truth.

In studies of abstract ideas, such as philosophy, the case for personal truth seems less clear. Impersonal abstractions are vital. Without them I could not write this book, nor could any of us speak or act or live. We depend on generalizing from the particu-lar, and in that movement we detach ourselves from personal truth. We cannot give up abstraction, but we need to recall and reclaim its personal roots. The generalizations on which we de-pend divorce us from life and from ourselves if we do not re-member their origins.

The great abstractions of our intellectual tradition arose from the passionate involvement of a knower with the world to be known. From Plato's ideas about form and substance, to Marx's theory of labor and value, to Einstein's $E = mc^2$, we find behind the generalization a person who allowed the world to speak to him at extraordinary depth. The problem of detachment comes as these ideas are studied generations away from their human origins, many steps removed from the personal quality of their source. Only later, as we recall the thought but forget the thinker, do we imagine a world of abstractions disassociated from the personal act of knowing.

An abstract idea is a word. Words are spoken by a human voice. When we study an idea we need first to treat it not as an abstraction but as a human sound. Our opening question should not be "How logical is that thought?" but "Whose voice is behind it? What is the personal reality from which that thought emerged? How can I enter and respond to the relation of that thinker to the world?" These questions do not exclude logic and critical intelligence, but they remind us that true knowing involves more than a disembodied intellect computing data. Knowledge of truth requires a personal dialogue between the knower and the known, a dialogue in which the knower listens to the world with obedience.

I realize that a mode of knowing that asks us to personify all that we know smacks of anthropomorphism, animism, *argumentum ad hominem*, and assorted other insults to the objectivist sensibility. But if we understand "the person" as the most objective reality (because of its capacity for self-definition and self-defense), the personal mode of knowing runs less risk than objectivism of diminishing reality to self-serving subjective terms. In a world devastated by the objectification of everything, including ourselves, this "primitive" way of personal knowing may turn out to be quite advanced. Perhaps we are ready now to see the wisdom of treating the known as a living self with whom we need to be in dialogue, rather than as an inert thing over which we can exercise our flawed mastery, our fatal control.[11]

Knowledge that personifies the known is consistent to the core with Christian spirituality. It was spiritual progress, not regress, when men and women understood that God had become a person and walked among us. The incarnation does not diminish God, does not reduce God to narrow human terms. Instead, it explodes the boundaries of the human enterprise; it infinitely enlarges the self and the world. "The world," says Gerard Manley Hopkins, "is charged with the grandeur of God," and this is the grandeur: not that the world is vast and incomprehensible, but that every "thing" in the world now possesses a personal name and the preciousness of personhood—every rock, every flower, every beast that crawls, every human self. In light of the incarnation, the world is no longer an object to be manipulated and owned. Instead, it is a community of persons, and knowing its truth means recovering the bonds of personhood and community that have been lost between us.

Obedience to Truth

What is the basic bond of the community of truth? What kind of relationship does truth call us into? As the story of Abba Felix suggests, the word that best applies is "obedience"—not slavish adherence to authority, but careful listening and responding in a conversation of free selves. Throughout the Scriptures, knowing and obedient listening are linked. Jesus says to Pilate, "Everyone who is of the truth hears my voice." He means that to be in the relationship called truth is to be able to listen and respond.

Elsewhere Jesus says, "If you continue in my word, you are truly my disciples, and you will know the truth, and the truth will make you free" (John 8:31). Here Jesus not only links knowing truth with obedience, but he also connects obedience with freedom. This connection is not simply a quirk of Christian teaching. The idea that freedom is achieved through obedience to truth is also at the heart of liberal education, whose aim is to liberate us through knowledge. Both our spiritual and our secular traditions affirm that truth will set us free, that only in obedience to truth can freedom be found.

But today we conceive of freedom and obedience as contradictory states. We regard freedom as the autonomy of the self-seeking self, the self cut loose from traditional and communal bonds, and we think of obedience as the act of slaves, not free persons. Suspicion of obedience is especially pronounced among the cultural minorities of our day, among groups such as blacks and women and Jews who will rightly ask, "Whose truth are we being told to obey?" These groups know what it means to live under other people's "truth" in an obedience not freely chosen but coerced.

Objectivism itself has made us suspicious of obedience; it sounds like one of those commitments that enforce subjective bias and distort the integrity of the world's autonomous objects. Objectivism first arose as a way of liberating us from biased and subjective "truth." But is it still a way toward freedom? I think not. Indeed, the logic of objectivism has contributed to the rise of authoritarian personalities and totalitarian societies, to the ascent of unfreedom. As Richard Gelwick points out, we are surrounded by ideologies that invite us to surrender ourselves to an objective interpretation of life, telling us that this interpretation is objectively true and that we bear no responsibility for it.[12]

In our effort to resist the tyranny of these objectivist ideologies, we have swung toward an equally tyranical subjectivism. Too many of us subscribe to a weak doctrine of pluralism, to the simple notion that truth looks different when viewed from different angles. Because this notion concedes diversity without calling us into dialogue, it leaves us in isolation and destroys community as effectively as the objectivism it seeks to resist. Eventually, this theory of relativity leads to a war of all against all where power, not truth, prevails. And the outcome of that war is merely a new form of the same domination and oppression that subjectivism set out to counter. If a pluralistic society is to survive and flourish, neither objectivism nor subjectivism will suffice, but only the concept of truth as troth.

If truth is personal and communal, then our search for truth—and truth's search for us— will neither actively suppress nor passively concede our differences, but will invite them to interact in faithful relationship. The world's diversity goes for beyond the differences between men and women, blacks and whites, Christians and Jews. These fade into insignificance compared with the differences between human beings and other beings in the community of truth—soils and rocks and forest beasts and stars. If our approach to knowing fails to invite the creative interaction of this radical pluralism—collapsing instead into objective imperalism or subjective relativism—then it is not an approach to truth, not a way of knowing that can recover the organic community of creation.

Here is where the bond of obedience, of respectful listening and faithful responding, becomes critical. In a pluralistic natural world, the way to truth is to give voice to mute objects and dumb beasts so that they can speak of their relatedness to our lives. In a pluralistic society, the way to truth is to listen attentively to diverse voices and views for the claims they make on us. The bond of listening holds the cosmic community together—careful, vulnerable listening for how things look from this standpoint and that and that, a listening that allows us not only to know the other but to be known from the other's point of view.

Objectivism tells the world what it is rather than listening to what it says about itself. Subjectivism is the decision to listen to no one except ourselves. But truth requires listening in obedience to each other, responding to what we hear, acknowledging and recreating the bonds of the community of troth.

At its root, the word "obedience" means not only "to listen" but "to listen from below." How fascinating that this is also the commonsense meaning of the word "understand," which suggests that we know something by "standing under" it. Both obedience and understanding imply submitting ourselves to something larger than any one of us, something on which we all depend. Both imply subjecting ourselves to the communal bonds of truth.

The objectivist will doubtless argue that the personal mode of knowing is dangerously subjective. But the complex of words and images I am exploring here opens up a new sense of what "subjective" knowledge might mean—for that word also means "to place under." In that sense of the word, I *am* arguing for a subjective conception of truth, a truth to which we must subject ourselves. Truth calls us to submit ourselves to the community of which we are a part, to fidelity to those bonds of troth in which our truth resides. This view *is* dangerous, for submission will transform us, require us to become something new. In truth our lives are no longer our own but belong to the whole community of creation.

The root meaning of "objective" is "to put against, to oppose." This is the danger of objectivism: it is a way of knowing that places us in an adversary relation to the world. By this view, we are not required to change so that the whole community might flourish; instead, the world must change to meet our needs. Indeed, objectivism has put us in an adversary relation to one another. The oppression of cultural minorities by a white, middle-class, male version of "truth" comes in part from the domineering mentality of objectivism. Once the objectivist has "the facts," no listening is required, no other points of view are needed. The facts, after all, are the facts. All that remains is to bring others into conformity with objective "truth."

The view that truth is personal leads neither to objective imperialism nor subjective relativism. Instead, truth is found as we are obedient to a pluralistic reality, as we engage in that patient process of dialogue, consensus seeking, and personal transformation in which all parties subject themselves to the bonds of communal troth. Such a way of knowing is more likely to bridge our gaps and divisions than drive us farther apart. Such a way of knowing can help heal us and our broken world.

5. To Teach Is to Create a Space . . .

The Meaning of Space

How can we translate the theory of personal truth into a practical pedagogy? How can we bring teachers, students, and their subjects face to face in a community of troth? How can we develop realistic ways of teaching and learning that move us toward obedience, freedom, and truth?

As I deal with these questions, I will use a definition of teaching that flows from the story of Abba Felix and from his spiritual tradition: *to teach is to create a space in which obedience to truth is practiced*. In this chapter I focus on the first part of the definition, asking what it means to "create a space." In the next chapter I take up the second part, asking how we can "practice obedience to truth" in the classroom.

Space is central to the spirituality of the desert fathers and mothers. Abba Felix and his fellow seekers left the crowded cities to meet truth in the desert, one of the most open and spare spaces on earth. They went there not only to enter an outer space free of the cities' clutter, but also to open up an inner space of heart and mind, free of inward noise. In desert emptiness the soul is able to settle on truth, to concentrate on that which is essential to salvation.

The centrality of space is also evident in Abba Felix's method of teaching. His students come to him with an urgent request for "a word"; they want their inner space filled with the sounds of authority. But Abba Felix does not give them the word they seek. Instead, he leads them into the vast space of silence, a wordless inner desert in which their mental constructs of reality wither and fall away. When Abba Felix breaks the silence, it is only to say "There are no more words nowadays," since the students have broken troth with the teachers and their teachings. Even with his words he makes more silence, more desert, more space. His purpose in all this is clear; he wants to create a space in which the bonds of troth can be rewoven, in which we can seek truth and truth can seek us.

Space may sound like a vague, poetic metaphor until we realize that it describes experiences of everyday life. We know what it means to be in a green and open field; we know what it means to be on a crowded rush-hour bus. On the crowded bus we lack space to breathe and think and be ourselves. But in an open field, we open up too; ideas and feelings arise within us; our knowledge comes out of hiding.

These experiences of physical space have parallels in our relations with others. On our jobs we know what it is to be pressed and crowded, our space diminished by the urgency of deadlines and the competitiveness of colleagues. But then there are times when deadlines disappear and colleagues cooperate, when everyone has the space to move, invent, and produce with energy and enthusiasm. With family and friends we know how it feels to have unreasonable demands placed upon us, to be boxed in by the expectations of those nearest to us. But then there are times when we feel accepted for who we are (or forgiven for who we are not), times when a spouse or a child or a friend gives us the space both to be and to become.

Similar experiences of crowding and space are found in education. To sit in a class where the teacher stuffs our minds with information, organizes it with finality, insists on having the answers while being utterly uninterested in our views, and forces us into a grim competition for grades—to sit in such a class is to experience a lack of space for learning. But to study with a teacher who not only speaks but listens, who not only gives answers but asks questions and welcomes our insights, who provides information and theories that do not close doors but open new ones, who encourages students to help each other learn—to study with such a teacher is to know the power of a learning space.

Openness, Boundaries, and Hospitality

A learning space has three major characteristics, three essential dimensions: openness, boundaries, and an air of hospitality. When we understand what each of these means, we can find specific methods to create the space for learning.

Openness is no more than the commonsense meaning of space. To create space is to remove the impediments to learning that we find around and within us, to set aside the barriers behind which we hide so that truth cannot seek us out. We not only "find" these obstacles around and within us; we often create them our-selves to evade the challenge of truth and transformation. So creating a learning space means resisting our own tendency to clutter up our consciousness and our classrooms.

One source of that tendency is our fear of appearing ignorant to others or to ourselves. Even though we are brought into edu-cation by ignorance, the fear of "not knowing" often leads us to pack the learning space with projections and pretensions. Teach-ers lecture longest when they are least sure of what they are doing; that is when they parse concepts without end, unwind the interminable and irrelevant "illustration." Students write the longest and most convoluted term papers when they do not know what to say; that is when they invoke more adjectives and adverbs than the average English sentence can support.

Even the desert teachers were tempted from time to time to fill the learning space with meaningless words. But these teachers not only taught their students; their students knew how to teach them. Here is the story of Evagrius, an early desert father who became a major theologian. When Evagrius first came to the de-sert from Alexandria,

> he made the mistake of lecturing to the brethren during a discus-sion on some matter; they let him finish, and then one of them

said, "We know, Father, that if you had stayed in Alexandria you would have become a great bishop . . . ," after which Evagrius was understandably quiet.[1]

The brothers knew, and Evagrius quickly learned, that desert education depends not on bishops who fill space with their words but on obedient listeners.

If we are to open space for knowing, we must be alert to our fear of not knowing and to our fearful tendency to fill the learning space. First, we must see that not knowing is simply the first step toward truth, that the anxiety created by our ignorance calls not for instant answers but for an adventure into the unknown. If we can affirm the search for truth as a continually uncertain journey, we may find the courage to keep the space open rather than packing it with pretense. Second, we must remember that we not only seek truth but that truth seeks us as well. When we become obsessed with our own seeking, we fill the space with methods and hypotheses and reports that may be mere diversions. But when we understand that truth is constantly seeking us, we have reason to open a space in which truth might find us out.

The openness of a space is created by the firmness of its *boundaries*. A learning space cannot go on forever; if it did, it would not be a structure for learning but an invitation to confusion and chaos. A space has edges, perimeters, limits. When those boundaries are violated—when the city creeps into the desert, or when we return to the city in body or mind—the quality of space is destroyed. We pay the price of these violations in our own society, deprived of desert knowledge by urban sprawl, by highways penetrating the wilderness, by the omnipresent media with their incessant news of the world. The teacher who wants to create an open learning space must define and defend its boundaries with care.

Not only will this keep the space open, it will also keep the students from fleeing that space. The openness of space—which is at first appealing to our jangled minds—soon becomes a threat. As the clutter falls away we realize how much we depend on clutter to keep our minds employed, to make them feel masterful. We do not want to face the barrenness that comes when our mind-made structures fail, so we run toward some distraction. If you doubt this, try creating a long silence in your classroom as Abba Felix did in his. Feel the anxieties that arise in you and your students alike, anxieties so powerful that fifteen seconds of silence is about as much as the typical group can tolerate!

The desert teachers knew these anxieties well. They knew that in the desert, before we encounter truth, we must first wrestle with the demons of untruth that arise in the silence, demons that come from our own need to manipulate and master truth rather than let truth transform us. "It was this aspect of warfare with demons that was called 'ascesis,' the 'hard work' of being a monk."[2] So the desert teachers disciplined themselves to stand their ground, to stay within the boundaries of the learning space so that truth might seek them out. One symbol of this discipline was the "cell" (often a hut or cave) in which these teachers lived:

> The cell was of central importance in their asceticism. "Sit in your cell and it will teach you everything," they said. The point was that unless a man could find God *here*, in this one place, his cell, he would not find him by going somewhere else.[3]

For this reason, many monks to this day make a "vow of stability" as part of their monastic life. With this vow, they renounce the temptation to believe that some other monastery would be a better place to learn and grow. For that temptation often arises just at the point where the true knowing begins, the point where we are forced to face our illusions. Good teachers know that discomfort and pain are often signs that truth is struggling to be born among us. Such teachers will not allow their students, or themselves, to flee from the "cell." They will hold the boundaries firm, and hold us all within them, so that truth can do its work.

But precisely because a learning space can be a painful place, it must have one other characteristic—*hospitality*.[4] Hospitality means receiving each other, our struggles, our newborn ideas with openness and care. It means creating an ethos in which the community of troth can form, the pain of truth's transformations be borne.

Hospitality is a central virtue of the desert teachers and of the monasteries they founded. It is a virtue central to the biblical tradition itself, where God is always using the stranger to introduce us to strangeness of truth. To be inhospitable to strangers or strange ideas, however unsettling they may be, is to be hostile to the possibility of truth; hospitality is not only an ethical virtue but an epistemological one as well.

So the classroom where truth is central will be a place where every stranger and every strange utterance is met with welcome. This may suggest a classroom lacking essential rigor, a place in which questions of true and false, right and wrong, are subordinated to making sure that everyone "has a nice day." But that would be a false understanding of hospitality. Hospitality is not an end in itself. It is offered for the sake of what it can allow, permit, encourage, and yield. A learning space needs to be hospitable not to make learning painless but to make the painful things possible, things without which no learning can occur— things like exposing ignorance, testing tentative hypotheses, challenging false or partial information, and mutual criticism of thought. Each of these is essential to obedience to truth. But none of them can happen in an atmosphere where people feel threatened and judged. Abba Felix challenged his students to the depth of their beings, but he did it in a context of ultimate hospitality that allowed them to receive his judgement and ask for his prayer.

I have been in some classrooms where people *seemed* to be pressing each other, asking hard questions, stripping off the veils of falsehood and illusion. But behind the appearances, something else was often going on. In an inhospitable classroom, many questions do not come out of honest not knowing. They are rhetorical or political questions, designed to score points with the teacher or against other students, questions asked not for truth's sake but for the sake of winning. In such a setting it is nearly impossible to reveal genuine ignorance—which means that genuine openness to learning is nearly impossible as well. Only in hospitable classrooms, where questions and answers do not need to be couched within the ground rules of a competitive game, can we come into troth with each other and encounter truth's transformations.

Physical, Conceptual, and Dramatic Space

Openness, boundaries, hospitality: how do we create a learning space with these qualities? I want to explore a few practical approaches I (and other teachers) have tried—not in the desert, but in the context of conventional education.

The most obvious approach is in the physical arrangement of the classroom. When the chairs are arranged facing the lectern, row upon row, the learning space is confined to a narrow alley of attention between each student and the teacher. Such an arrangement speaks. It says that in this space there is no room for students to relate to each other and each other's thoughts; there is no invitation to a community of troth; there is no hospitality. But when the chairs are placed in a circle, creating an open space between us, within which we can connect, something else is said. The teacher may sit in that circle and talk, but we are all being invited to create a community of learning by engaging the ideas and one another in the open space between. I imagine Abba Felix teaching this way—sitting with his students in a circle on the sand, letting the little piece of desert between them represent the larger space in which they met, letting their own circle represent the boundaries from which they could not flee.

The teacher can also create a space with words—conceptual space we might call it—in at least two ways. One is through assigned reading; the other is through lecturing. I want to show first how reading assignments can open rather than close the learning space.

In the monastic communities which began with the desert teachers, reading is one of the fundamental disciplines of the learning life. But it is different from the sort of reading we do in school, not only in its content but in its method. Where schools give students several hundred pages of text and urge them to learn "speed reading," the monks dwell on a page or a passage or a line for hours and days at a time. They call it *lectio divina*, sacred reading, and they do it at a contemplative pace. This method allows reading to open, not fill, our learning space.

When all students in the room have read the same brief piece in a way that allows them to enter and occupy the text, a common space is created in which students, teacher, and subject can meet. It is an open space since a good text will raise as many questions as it answers. It is a bounded space since the text itself dictates the limits of our mutual inquiry. It is a hospitable, reassuring space since everyone has walked around in it beforehand and become acquainted with its dimensions. Too often we fail to capitalize on this space-creating quality of assigned reading. We assign readings of such length that they cannot contain a disciplined discussion. We hold students individually accountable for what they read on tests, but we seldom allow their reading to create a common space in which the group can meet in mutual accountability for their learning.

There is often need for longer reading assignments to gather background information and perspectives, but a shorter text can become the arena of focused exploration. The "text" might be a passage from an historical document, a scene from a novel, a poem or a piece of music. It might be a body of scientific data, the findings of an experiment, or a sociological survey. In each case, the teacher invites the students to step inside the space created by the text, asking them what is going on in it, how it can be understood, how they understand themselves within it. The key to this approach is to keep the students firmly within the boundaries of the text, to keep them from fleeing into ungrounded opinion, wishful thinking, or irrelevant facts. Let the text become our monastic cell. Let us sit there so that truth can seek us out.

For example, in teaching a course on the nature of compassion, I sometimes use a story by Martin Buber called "The Angel and the World's Dominion."⁵ The story begins:

> There was a time when the Will of the Lord, Whose hand has the
> power to create and destroy all things, unleashed an endless
> torrent of pain and sickness over all the Earth.

It goes on to tell of an angel who, saddened by the world's
plight, sought and received power from God to set things
straight. For a year the earth flourished, but when the people
harvested their prolific fields and made bread from the grain, "it
fell to pieces, and the pieces were unpalatable; they filled the
mouth with a disgusting taste, like clay." The distraught angel
returned to God: "Help me to understand where my power and
judgment were lacking." And God said:

> Behold a truth which is known to me, and only to me from the
> beginning of time, a truth too deep and dreadful for your deli-
> cate, generous hands, my sweet apprentice—it is this, that the
> Earth must be nourished with putrefaction and covered with
> shadows that its seeds may bring forth—and it is this, that souls
> must be made fertile with flood and sorrow, and through them
> the Great Work may be born.

There is much about this story, this learning space, that my
students find confining and uncomfortable. They do not like the
idea of a God who can and does create woe. They do not like the
fact that the angel's best efforts are defeated by some inexorable
law. But I try to hold my students within the boundaries of the
world the story describes. The slippery subject of "compassion"
becomes less elusive as we pursue it within that delimited world;
and the subject pursues us as we are forced to say how our own
experience of compassion compares to the angel's.

A teacher can also create a learning space by means of lectures.
By providing critical information and frameworks of interpretation, a lecturer can lay down the boundaries within which learning occurs—but not if the lecturer uses words to fill up space, as
too many do. The teacher who offers a single body of data and
omits competing evidence closes the learning space. The teacher

who gives a single interpretation of the data rather than suggesting alternate theories fails to open a space in which students are
challenged to learn.

I have heard of a history teacher who knew how to open space
with a lecture—and who exemplifies the courage it takes to do
so. At the first class, this teacher gave a detailed lecture surveying
the major events of the period under consideration. At the end of
that session, with the students bending under the weight of information the teacher had dumped on them, he said: "You can
tear up all your notes because much of what I said today is un-
true. Some of it was so patently false you should have been
suspicious—there was no electrical power in the seventeenth
century! From time to time in the coming term I will slip in more
lies. It will be up to you to catch them, and to challenge me if you
want to get things straight. I will not accept any of my own lies as
answers on exams. They are false even if I *did* say them. Class
dismissed."

Whether that story is true or not (and I am not going to say), it
shows how a lecturer can open a learning space. I imagine that
this class became a model of attentive listening and challenging
questioning. This teacher created a space in which students
learned that truth is not a result of authoritative pronouncement
but of personal and corporate discernment, a space in which students became dependent on each other to spot the fallacies, a
space that not only invited but compelled students to participate
in their own and each other's education.

It is not accidental, I think, that this same technique, was used
on occasion by the desert teachers themselves:

> One of the brethren related this. "One day I went to . . . see
> Abba Joseph. Now in the monastery there was a very good mul-
> berry tree. At early dawn he said to me, 'Go and eat.' But as it
> was Friday, I did not go, because of the [required] fast; so I asked
> him, 'For God's sake, explain this to me. Here you are saying to
> me, go and eat but I did not go, because of the fast. I blushed for
> shame thinking of your command. I asked myself what was the
> old man's intention in saying that and I wondered if I ought to

have done it, since he told me to.' The old man said, 'At the beginning the Fathers do not speak to the brothers as they ought to, but rather in an ambiguous manner, and if they see that they do what is right, then they no longer speak like that, but tell them the truth when they know they are obedient in all things.'"[6]

These stories illustrate the role of drama in opening up a space for learning. I do not mean the drama created by the teacher's charisma or ability as an actor. Few of us have such gifts; to advocate a mode of teaching that requires them is to defeat us before we begin (notwithstanding the tragicomic fact that some faculties have hired professional scriptwriters and comedians to "enliven" their lectures!). No, the dramatic space on which teaching depends is that created by the claims of truth on our lives. All of us can learn to lecture in ways that create dramatic tension—if only by telling our students we will lie from time to time. In this way we remind our students that there is a rule of truth that governs us—the rule of fasting that overrode Abba Joseph's commands, the rule of historical veracity and common sense that overrode the history teacher's false claims. The gap between that rule and our perceptions creates a dramatic space into which our students can be drawn, a space where they can learn the skills of discernment and mutual truth-telling.

The dramatic space I am talking about is found in the evolution of the theater from the proscenium stage to the theater-in-the-round. I am not suggesting that teachers should be actors on stage, mesmerizing an audience that sits "out there" and learns to "theorize" the world from afar. Instead, I am calling for teachers who bring the audience into the play, who create the space that draws students, teacher, and subject alike into truth's own drama.

Silence and Speech

In addition to the space created by the arrangement of the classroom and common readings and lectures, there are other ways for teachers to make room for truth. Here I want to explore two of them: the kind of speech we utter, and the silence from which true speech comes.

Speech is a precious gift and a vital tool, but too often our speaking is an evasion of truth, a way of buttressing our self-serving reconstructions of reality. So silence, as we have seen, was essential to the desert teachers. In silence more than in argument our mind-made world falls away and we are opened to the truth that seeks us. If our speech is to become more truthful it must emerge from and be corrected by the silence that is its source.

I often begin my classes with a period of silence. It may last only a few minutes, but it gives us a chance to settle in and center down, to move a bit beyond the truth-evading distractions of our minds and emotions. I do not call this practice "prayer," but that is what it is—a time when we can still ourselves enough to begin to feel our natural connectedness to each other and the world.

I also use periods of silence in the middle of a class, especially in an open discussion when the words start to tumble out upon each other and the problem we are trying to unravel is getting more tangled. I try to help my students learn to spot those moments and settle into a time of quiet reflection in which the knots might come untied. We need to abandon the notion that "nothing is happening" when it is silent, to see how much new clarity a silence often brings.

Sometimes I use a simple rule that allows these silences to occur naturally instead of requiring my intervention. I merely ask that a student not speak more than twice (or three times in an emergency) in the course of an hour's conversation. The results are quite remarkable. Because of the pauses, the slowed pace, many more people speak than do in the normal free-for-all discussion. The more aggressive and verbal students (the twenty percent who usually dominate eighty percent of the talk) are checked and reined. They are forced to sort and sift what they have to say, looking for that which is essential. The quieter, more retiring students suddenly find the space to speak. They also feel a new responsibility to speak; no longer do they have the luxury of letting the more impetuous ones pull the load. Often I discover that students who say little in fast-paced discussion have gifts of deep insight—perhaps because they have been forced to spend most of their lives quietly thinking things over.

In most places where people meet, silence is a threatening experience. It makes us self-conscious and awkward; it feels like some kind of failure. So the teacher who uses silence must understand that a silent space seems inhospitable at first to people who measure progress by noise. Silence must be introduced cautiously; we must allow ourselves to be slowly re-formed in its discipline before it can become an effective teaching tool. But once the use of silence is established with a group, once we learn that we make progress in being quiet (and if we fall back, it is only because our previous progress was illusory), then silence becomes a potent space for learning.

Eventually my students feel a sense of community in the silence that is deeper than what they feel when the words are flowing fast and hard. Words so often divide us, but silence can unite. In the silence we are more likely to sense the unity of truth which lies beneath our overanalyzed world, the relatedness between us and others and the world we inhabit and study. When we emerge from silence with this sense of unity in our hearts, it is easier to speak and hear words of troth.

What about our words? What kind of speech can we utter to create a space for truth? Through the discipline of silence I have learned how often my words are uttered to fill space rather than open it up. So often, I speak to solve problems for people, to give them definitive answers to their questions. Frequently, I rush to respond in order to prove my authority or relieve a moment of classroom tension. I forget that tension can be creative; I fail to give it a chance to draw us into the learning space. I do not allow my students' problems and questions to deepen within them, to do their own educative work. I forget that genuine solutions and authentic answers can only come from within my students, that to "educate" them I must speak words that draw out their under-

standing rather than impose my own. Even the facts and theories
I must speak will not be absorbed if they are not spoken into the
receptiveness of a compelling question.

So I have learned in the silence that it is often better to speak a
question than an answer. It is natural that silence should teach us
to ask questions, since silence is a question itself. In the silence I
have learned to ask questions that open up a space where students can listen to their own experience, to each other, and to the
subject at hand—not merely to the authority of the teacher.
Teaching by questioning was the genius of Socrates, of Jesus, and
of Abba Felix as well. Only after letting the silence question his
students, and only after asking his students a question to reveal
them to themselves ("You wish to hear a word?"), was Abba
Felix able to lead them to the edge of truth.

For a model of education by questioning, I reach beyond conventional education to a Quaker practice called "the clearness
committee." Quakers (whose spirituality is steeped in silence and
premised on the belief that truth is always seeking us out) first
used these committees to offer counsel to couples who wished to
be married. Today the practice has been extended to anyone who
needs help in thinking through a problem or decision. I believe
that the clearness committee can also be adapted to classroom
use.

The process begins with the couple or individual writing out
the question or problem along with the background information.
The couple, let us say, then recruit a committee of five or six,
share the written material with them, and together they sit down
to talk things over. But the talk is governed by a firm ground
rule: committee members are not to offer their own answers or
solutions to the issue at hand. They are confined to asking questions—which the couple answer in the presence of the group.
The answers generate more questions, the questions generate
more answers, and both questions and answers deepen as the
meeting goes one.

The process sounds simple, and it is. But it is also demanding
in its discipline and startling in its results. It demands that we

abandon our habit of giving advice and answers when someone brings a question our way; it demands that we learn to listen. The process is startling because as it goes on it usually becomes clear that the individual or couple have had their own inner answer all along, that the questions simply serve to uncover and reveal it. This is "education" in the root sense of the word—drawing out the learners' truth. Couples in the rush of romance often discover that they had failed to ask each other some of the hard questions on which a good marriage depends; sometimes they learn that they are not ready to marry after all. People facing hard vocational decisions find that they have inner guidance on which way to go. Within the space of caring but incisive questioning, truth is given room to make itself known.

I can imagine various ways to adapt the clearness committee to classroom use. Suppose the problem at hand were the meaning of a body of data. Ordinarily, the teacher would either tell the students what the data mean or pit the students against one another in a competition for the fullest and fastest interpretation. An alternative is to organize students into small groups, with one person taking the role of problem-presenter while the others act as interrogators. Using the simple rules of the clearness process, a great deal of mutual teaching and learning will go on, bringing students and subject into the community of truth.

I do not suggest that questions are the only educative sort of speech. Our facts and theories, our advice and answers need to be spoken as well. But since we as teachers are overschooled to give answers and solutions, and since we give them for reasons as often evasive as educative, we have special need to develop the discipline of asking questions to create a space for truth.

Making Space for Feelings

I have spoken so far of creating cognitive space, space that allows evidence and insight to emerge. But teachers must also create emotional space in the classroom, space that allows feelings to arise and be dealt with. We often clutter our learning space with obstacles and distractions to evade the emotions that education evokes. If we leave those emotions unattended, we will not be able to clear that space. Fear of feelings—and especially the feeling of fear—are major barriers to creating the space this sort of teaching requires.

Space itself is often frightening. Students are threatened by an open invitation to learn for themselves and to help each other learn; they would much rather have their education packaged and sold by the teacher. They are threatened by the strangeness of what they do not know, by the thought of having to expose their ignorance, by having to relate to their peers in ways that would hardly occur to them outside the classroom, and by the possibility of a failure that will mar their self-esteem and careers. Students come into a classroom with these fears close to the surface. If they are not acknowledged and addressed they will close down the space for learning.

But teachers, too, enter the classroom with fears; at least I do. I am afraid of being inadequately prepared, of having my own ignorance exposed, of meeting the glazed eyes and bored expressions of some of my students. Behind my role and my expertise, I wonder what they think about me as a person. They may be afraid of my power over their lives, the power of the grade and credential, but I am afraid of the negative or ambivalent feelings my power creates in them. I need their affirmation as much as they need mine; I need a sense of community with them that our roles make tenuous.

The standard advice to teachers, at least by implication, is: "Never show the students you are afraid, or you will lose control." There may be situations in which that is true, but I have never taught in one. On the contrary, the kind of teaching I am exploring here demands that we "lose control" so that truth can control us. Creating a learning space that is not closed down by fearful emotions requires a teacher who is not afraid of feelings.

The teacher must make the first move in opening the space for feelings simply because the teacher has the power to do so. In whatever way seems natural, the teacher needs to convey something like this to the students: "This is the place where it is safe for your feelings to emerge. I have feelings too, and I will make myself vulnerable by telling you some of them. Teaching and learning are human enterprises, and we must use human emotions in the learning process rather than letting them use us. I will take the lead in this so that you will feel encouraged to follow. I will try to respond to your feelings with an understanding that comes from knowing my own."

I am not suggesting that a class be turned into a therapy group. But I am suggesting that sensitivity to feelings is essential to this kind of teaching and learning—not only because submerged feelings can undermine learning, but also because feelings are a part of the whole person: we can enter into the relationship called truth only in our wholeness, not with our minds alone. Indeed, our feelings may be more vital to truth than our minds, since our minds strive to analyze and divide things while our feelings reach for relatedness. Even the feeling of fear that teachers and students bring to class is an obverse sign of our emotional need for community. Our fears arise from the sense that community is not present or possible, that we are not related to each other in a way that allows us to be vulnerable without being damaged. By dealing with those fears we begin to sense the mutual need for community that lies behind them, and sensing that need we are better able to open ourselves to the community that is truth.

I use several simple devices to make space for the feelings that help weave community, devices that do not involve the pretense that I am a therapist. I usually begin a course with extended self-introductions, asking my students to respond to queries about themselves that go beyond the surface statistics. Feelings will not be expressed and community will not form until we know each other and feel known in certain elemental ways. When self-introductions are omitted it is a clear signal that in this class only the teacher and the subject will have a chance to be known, that the subjective experience of the student is of no account.

When it comes time for me to introduce myself, I often speak about the mixed emotions of excitement and anxiety I have at the outset of a new class. I may try to identify with my students by recollecting my own feelings when I was in the student role. I may invite them to speak with me, in or out of class, about the emotions that the course generates in them.

During a class session, I try to stay aware of my students' feelings and respond accordingly. If a timid student contributes some information or insight that seems wildly off the mark, I try to redirect it toward the target rather than let it fly astray. In such a case I seldom find it fitting simply to say "Wrong. You missed." Instead, I try to engage the student in dialogue to help improve his or her aim. I try to remember, too, how vulnerable many students feel when they merely ask a question, and I keep in mind the example of a great teacher, Leo Strauss, as described by his one-time student Werner Dannhauser:

> He encouraged questions, and I suspect he would have agreed with Heidegger that questioning is the piety of thinking. . . . I remember the first time I asked him something about Hobbes. I thought I was being stupid and I was afraid of exposing my stupidity, but he set up situations where one learned not to be afraid to admit that, or what, one did not understand. So I asked, and he astonished me by raising my questions to a stratospheric level. I had not known what I was asking, but I was wrestling with a genuine perplexity. I remember his leaving his desk. . . and coming over to my chair, talking to me personally about some knotty problem in Hobbes. . . [and] before he was through I had learned something about what it meant to think.[7]

At the end of a class session, I may take ten or fifteen minutes for a corporate evaluation of how the class went. At first these discussions are brief and awkward; students are accustomed to evaluating a class privately with each other, not with the teacher in public. But as we grow easier with the practice, these evaluations help to clear out the learning space. Sometimes they alert us to cognitive issues—a certain point has been understood by only half the group. But more often they allow feelings to emerge. For example, people may speak of the frustration they felt in trying to get in on a discussion. Perhaps the men in the class dominated, leaving the women out. Evaluations like this tend to contain their own solutions. When everyone knows that the next session will end with another evaluation, the verbose ones generally need few reminders to make room for others to speak.

Paying attention to feelings may seem "soft" to tough-minded teachers. But as I create space for feelings, I find that the group's capacity for tough-mindedness grows. The methods are simple but tricky; one has to watch for our tendency to want to deal more with familiar feelings than with the alien subject at hand. But properly employed, with an eye to the end of learning, methods such as these increase our ability to expose our own ignorance, to ask hard questions, to challenge the validity of what others are saying and receive similar challenges in a spirit of growth. Few of these things will happen in a space choked off by repressed emotions. But in an emotionally honest learning space, one created by a teacher who does not fear feelings and who uses some simple techniques, the community of truth can flourish between us and we can flourish in it.

6.   . . . In Which Obedience to Truth Is Practiced

The Rule of Truth

"To teach is to create a space in which obedience to truth is practiced." Now I turn to the second part of that definition. As we create a space for learning, how do we practice obedience to truth within it?

In conventional education, the classroom is not regarded as a place to "practice" anything. Practice goes on in the world, and the classroom is a place set apart. Practice is what students are being prepared for—it is oriented toward the future. Their preparation consists of absorbing accumulated knowledge—it is oriented to the past. So the realities that concern conventional education are "out there" in the world, "back there" in the past, and "up there" in the future. The most neglected reality in education is the reality of the present moment, of what is happening here and now in the classroom itself.

To speak of the classroom as a place "in which obedience to truth is practiced" is to break the barriers between the classroom and the world—past, present, and future. To speak this way is to affirm that what happens in the classroom *is* happening in the world; the way we relate to each other and our subject reflects and shapes the way we conduct our relationships in the world. By this definition of teaching, we practice troth between knowers and the known in the classroom itself.

The class is understood as part of the community of truth—more intense and reflective perhaps than other parts of that community, but related to all the rest. Reality is no longer "out there" but between us; we bridge the gap between learning and living by attending to the living reality of the learning situation. In such a class neither knowing nor living can become a spectator sport, for the class itself calls us to the same involvement and accountability to which we are called by truth. The classroom becomes the microcosm of a world governed by the rule of truth. In it we learn both to know and to live under that rule.

This notion of "the rule of truth" is critical, for the teaching of personal truth always runs the risk of reducing truth to private perceptions, interpretations, and feelings. This sort of teaching must have some equivalent to the rules of scientific inquiry, a process and a set of standards by which we can both make and measure progress toward the community of truth. The process and standards must embrace the rules of logic and evidence, thus saving the best of objectivity, while going beyond them to save the best of subjectivity as well—the sense that we and the world we study are not autonomous "things" but interdependent beings, subject to truth's claims.

My task in this chapter is not to supercede the scientific method —for which I am grateful! Instead, I am looking for the rule of truth in teaching, a rule that can order our inquiries and bring us all, knowers and knowns, into mutually obedient relationships of troth.

The Complexities of Obedience

The key to the rule of truth in teaching and learning is found in that word "obedience," which means to listen with a discerning ear and respond faithfully to the personal implications of what one has heard. Obedience does not mean slavish, mechanical adherence to whatever one hears; it means making a personal response that acknowledges that one is in troth with the speaker and with the words he or she speaks. Abba Felix was an obedient teacher precisely because he did *not* succumb to his students' demand for "a word." Instead, he was obedient to the truth he heard within that plea, to the fact that his students wanted verbal diversions from truth's claims on their lives. So Abba Felix told

them "There are no more words nowadays," and he told them
why. By being obedient to the brokenness of the relation between teacher and students, he revealed that brokenness to the
students themselves and brought them deeper into the community called truth.

Leslie Dewart, offers a partial clue to the nature of obedience
to truth. Truth, he says,

> is a *fidelity* rather than a *conformity*. What is the difference be-
> tween the two? *Conformity* is a relation towards another which is
> owing to another by reason of the other's nature. *Fidelity* is a
> relation towards another which one owes to oneself by reason of
> one's own nature. Conformity obligates from the outside. Fidelity
> . . . obligates from within.[1]

In the personal mode of knowing and teaching we must always be aware of the other's nature. But that nature—which is
sometimes darkened by ignorance or prejudice or greed—is not
the final arbiter of our response. We must respond to the other
not in conformity to what he or she wants, but in fidelity or
obedience to the truth within us. Of course, our own nature may
be as dark as the other's. So we must allow the other to speak
back to us, not in conformity to what we want to hear, but in
fidelity to the other's truth. The truth we are seeking, the truth
that seeks us, lies ultimately in the community of being where
we not only know but are known.

This process of dialogue, where each person speaks in fidelity
to inner truth rather than conformity to outward demands, is a
process of checking and criticizing and clarifying our communal
relationships. It is a quest for truth as troth. As the dialogue goes
on, a larger truth is revealed, a truth that is not only within us but
between us. It is the truth that we are not autonomous agents,
each with a private world, but are in community with each other.
Community begins to emerge as we seek our inward nature. But
it can grow only as we realize that our created nature calls us into
obedient relationship with each other and all that we know; it

can grow only as our inward response finds outward manifestation in relationships of dialogue and troth.

Obedience to relational truth is obviously a tricky business. Some of its ambiguities have been described by Dietrich Bonhoeffer in an essay called "Telling the Truth." Because Bonhoeffer not only wrote about these things but obediently followed truth to his death at the hands of the Nazis, his words about the complications of truth telling have special weight for me:

> "Telling the truth" . . . is not solely a matter of moral character; it is also a matter of correct appreciation of real situations and of serious reflection upon them. The more complex the actual situations of a man's [or woman's] life, the more responsible and the more difficult will be his task of "telling the truth."
>
> For example, a teacher asks a child in front of the class whether it is true that his father often comes home drunk. It is true, but the child denies it. . . . He feels . . . that what is taking place is an unjustified interference in the order of the family, and that he must oppose it. What goes on in the family is not for the ears of the class in school. . . . As a simple no to the teacher's question the child's answer is certainly untrue; yet at the same time it nevertheless gives expression to the truth that the family is an institution *sui generis* and that the teacher has no right to interfere with it. The child's answer can indeed by called a lie; yet this lie contains more truth, that is to say, it is more in accordance with reality than would have been the case if the child had betrayed his father's weakness in front of the class.[2]

That scene speaks to me about obedience to truth in teaching for several reasons. It reminds me that the questions I ask my students must take into account the larger community of truth in which they live their lives. It reminds me that many relationships of troth are present in the classroom, that I must sense and respect that troth in order to teach, and that my teaching will strengthen and enlarge my students' relationships only as I enter them with care. Bonhoeffer also suggests that I must occasionally "lie" in the name of truth, of the troth that exists between my students and me, that my students may not come into truth if I use the sledgehammer of fact ("You are dead wrong in what you just said"), and that I need to speak to them in that love without which truth cannot be known.

But Bonhoeffer's tale also makes me yearn for a classroom that does not trap students the way that child was caught. The child needs a learning place in which he does not have to "lie," a place where the dark facts of his life can be illumined by the process of education. Again, I am not proposing that the class become a therapy group. I do not mean that the teacher should drop the lesson for the day and try to work out the child's problem. But unless the classroom can somehow embrace the relations and struggles of students' lives, students will continue to "lie" to teachers, to separate the learning process from the rest of their lives. At best, such an education continually flounders on the students' hidden personal agendas. At worst, it creates a kind of schizophrenia in which knowing runs on one track, living on another, and never do the two tracks meet.

Practicing obedience to truth in the classroom is complex and confusing. We can begin only by steeping ourselves in the idea of obedience, by understanding that obedience is not a mechanical kind of truth telling but a sensitive process of feeling for the troth that exists between students and teachers, our subject and our world. There are no sure-fire "how to do it" techniques, but there are some practical pedagogies that serve the purpose better than others. I want to share my experience with a few of these methods.

Learning by Consensus

I found one model for practicing obedience to truth in a most unlikely place—a simulation game called "Lost on the Moon."[3] In the game, students are posed with an objective problem to be solved. They are to imagine that they belong to the crew of a spaceship that has crash-landed on the moon's surface. They are

given a list of fifteen items of equipment that survived the crash—a map of the lunar constellations, several gallons of water, a compass, oxygen tanks, a length of rope, and so on. Two hundred miles from the crash site another spaceship waits to take them back to earth. The goal is to move the crew from the crash to the rescue ship by using the surviving equipment.

The students' task is to rank each of the fifteen items of equipment according to its usefulness in making that trip. First they are asked to rank the items privately, drawing upon whatever knowledge they possess that bears on the problem at hand. Then they are brought together in groups of six or eight to discuss their individual rankings, to negotiate their differences, and to arrive at a corporate ranking—a *consensus* decision about the relative utility of the various pieces of equipment.

Although it is only a game, "Lost on the Moon" has one feature that makes it a valid educational model: successful completion of the task requires knowledge, not opinion. Does a compass work on the moon? What is the moon's surface gravity and how will it affect the crew's movement and the use of certain equipment? How useful would it be to know the lunar constellations? Since most groups playing the game do not include an astrophysicist, the group must find a way to sort and sift partial knowledge, hunches, and opinions to distinguish true from false claims.

When a group has reached consensus, the item rankings of both individuals and the group are compared to expert rankings provided by the National Aeronautics and Space Administration. These comparisons yield numerical scores, measures of the success with which both individuals and the group performed their task. Individual scores range all over the map, since some students have more relevant knowledge than others, but when these individual scores are compared with the group score, the results are frequently remarkable.

The group score is almost always higher than the average of individual scores, which suggests that the process of reaching consensus raises a group's knowledge above the average knowl-

edge of its members. But even more significant, the group score is often better than the best individual score in the group, which suggests that through consensus the group can achieve a level of knowledge higher than that of the group's most knowledgeable member. The extent of these differences depends entirely on the quality of the group process. When a group has been specially trained in learning by consensus, these differences are dramatically increased.

What is going on here? Through consensual inquiry, people are learning by "practicing obedience to truth"; that is, they are learning by listening and responding faithfully to each other and to the subject at hand. They are using an educational process that is not individualized and competitive but communal and cooperative, one that reflects the communal nature of reality itself. They are learning by practicing the rule of truth as troth.

This rule first brings us into obedience to one another; it guides us in a process of group discussion and discernment. But then it brings us into obedience with the subject at hand. The obedience we practice to one another becomes obedience to a reality beyond us that has an "objective" nature. As we listen to each other, we hear various versions of that reality, and as those versions confirm and contradict each other we move toward a consensus with each other that is more faithful to the reality beyond us.

The consensual process of truth seeking is based on the simple assumption that all of us thinking together are smarter than any one of us thinking alone—as the scores often demonstrate. Through consensus we transform the fragmentary knowledge of individuals into a knowledge more complete, a transformation that occurs as students enter into obedience to each other and to the subject at hand. The knowledge of the group as a whole is not merely additive; it is always potentially greater than the sum of its parts.

But what is good consensual process? What are the rules of truth that govern this sort of inquiry? What kind of practical training is required for a group to practice obedience to truth? A

suggestive sketch has been provided by Jay Hall, the author of "Lost on the Moon." He studied the interactions of groups who played the game most effectively and came up with these rules for seeking truth by consensus, the rules of truth as troth:

> Consensus is a decision process for making full use of available resources and for resolving conflicts creatively. Consensus is difficult to reach, so not every ranking will meet with everyone's *complete* approval. Complete unanimity is not the goal—it is rarely achieved. But each individual should be able to accept the group rankings on the basis of logic and feasibility. When all group members feel this way, you have reached consensus as defined here, and the judgment may be entered as a group decision. This means, in effect, that a single person can block the group if he thinks it necessary; at the same time, he should use this option in the best sense of reciprocity. Here are some guidelines to use in achieving consensus:
>
> 1. Avoid arguing for your own rankings. Present your position as lucidly and logically as possible, but listen to the other members' reactions and consider them carefully before you press your point.
>
> 2. Do not assume that someone must win and someone must lose when discussion reaches a stalemate. Instead, look for the next-most-acceptable alternative for all parties.
>
> 3. Do not change your mind simply to avoid conflict and to reach agreement and harmony. When agreement seems to come too quickly and easily, be suspicious. Explore the reasons and be sure everyone accepts the solution for basically similar or complementary reasons. Yield only to positions that have objective and logically sound foundations.
>
> 4. Avoid conflict-reducing techniques such as majority votes, averages, coin-flips and bargaining. When a dissenting member finally agrees, don't feel that he must be rewarded by having his own way on some later point.
>
> 5. Differences of opinion are natural and expected. Seek them out and try to involve everyone in the decision process. Disagreements can help the group's decision because with a wide range of information and opinions, there is a greater chance that the group will hit upon more adequate solutions.[4]

It is important to note the creative role of conflict in this process. Individual perceptions of reality differ; to enter troth with each other and with reality means exposing those differences openly and honestly so that they can inform and reshape one another. In this kind of learning process, students are urged to speak with the courage of their convictions, but in the process, they open their convictions to correction and change. When we learn by consensus, we are no longer subject to the tyranny of either objective authoritarianism or subjective relativism. Instead, we enter into the mutuality and relatedness of reality itself, and our knowledge grows as we listen and respond to the complexities of the community of truth.

In his research Jay Hall also found that the consensus process, with its emphasis on creative conflict, works best in groups whose members are comfortable with one another—confirmation for the claim that a hospitable learning space allows us to bear the painful parts of learning:

> Differences of opinion are not likely to be seen as particularly threatening to a group that is already well established. Disagreements are seen as natural; they indicate a need for further discussion and offer a variety of alternative solutions, but they don't imply interpersonal hostility or threaten the integrity of the group.
>
> But in a group of semistrangers the situation is different. Here there is no group commitment, and the cohesion is tenuous and temporary. Conflict threatens the group's already flimsy interpersonal structure, thus members try to smooth conflicts over rather than resolve them. When disagreement arises, the members of an ad-hoc group make quick compromises to get along with each other, or they result to neutral, automatic solutions, such as majority rule.[5]

Some readers may be tempted to say, "But this is only a game. It has little to do with other kinds of learning." I disagree. The consensual process that allows students to solve this imaginary problem is the same process that allows a class to enter the deepest truth of a piece of literature or a poem. It is the same process that enables students to find the meaning of a set of sociological statistics or a body of historical data. It is, indeed, the same process employed by the scientific community at large. In all of these cases, facts are gathered, knowledge is shared, interpretations are tested against one another, and from the conflicts of data and interpretations a fuller knowledge emerges.

Consensus is the practical process by which we practice obedience and troth. Consensus is not a democracy of opinion in which a majority vote equals truth. Instead, it is a process of inquiry in which the truth that emerges through listening and responding to each other and the subject at hand is more likely to transcend collective opinion than fall prey to it. With consensus, individual truth is both affirmed and corrected by the communal troth in which we live and learn. With consensus, the learning process itself becomes a model of the obedience required for us to live faithfully with each other and our common world. Students who learn in this way are learning more than facts. They are learning a way of relating obediently to each other and to their world; they are practicing a communal epistemology that will form them in a communal ethic.

Some teachers who are attracted to this sort of corporate learning will despair of using it because of the size of their classes. How can a class of one hundred or more practice consensual learning? If one proposes that such classes be broken into smaller discussion groups, teachers will complain that these groups turn quickly into undisciplined "rap sessions" where little learning goes on. But the virtue of the consensual process is that it has definable rules, and students can learn to use its disciplines by themselves.

In larger classes I train students for small group work in a way that resists the tendency toward "rapping." First we discuss the rules of consensus seeking. Then I ask a small group of students to work on a problem, using those rules, in the presence of the entire class. When they finish I ask the class to comment on the group process they have just observed. Were the rules honored? Where were they stretched or broken? What happened at those moments, and how can we avoid repeating them? Then I may select another small group and go through the process again, to refine it even further. In this way the class gains competence in consensus, and when we break into small self-led groups there is enough leadership to go around. Though the chance of aimless conversation is not eliminated, it is minimized—especially when each group is asked to report on its process and outcomes to me.

The Voice of the Subject

In every classroom there are really three parties to the conversation: the teacher, the students, and the subject itself. Though the importance of this third party is implicit in what I have said about consensus (we do not solve the problem of being "lost on the moon" without attending to lunar realities) it needs to be made more explicit. The practice of obedience to truth requires not only that we listen to one another but also to the subject at hand. We need to find ways to give that subject a voice of its own, a voice that can speak its own truth and resist our tendency to reduce it to our terms. In part, of course, this happens as I listen to the voices of others in the classroom whose perceptions of the subject differ from mine. But the subject itself has a voice. To practice obedience to truth we must strain to hear what the subject is saying about itself beyond all our interpretations.

This sort of attentive listening is precisely what is going on in a scientific laboratory. Though the scientist uses certain instruments to amplify the subject's voice, he or she is continually trying to hear those faint noises of nature the instruments can barely pick up. When such signals are received, however dimly, the scientist knows that the problem is in the receiver, that we must develop more attentive ways of listening to nature's voice lest we suppress or distort it.

The same insistence on careful listening is found in the story of the history professor who lied to his class. That teacher was saying to his students: "There is a voice of historical authenticity which speaks beyond my own words. Listen for it, and hold us all accountable to what you hear."

In my own teaching I find that the autonomy of the subject's voice grows as I move my students beyond "looking at" the subject into personal dialogue with it. When we simply look at a subject we tend to impose our private perceptions on it; we lose the sense that the subject has a reality of its own. But when we interview the subject instead of just viewing it, then we find the subject speaking back to us in ways surprisingly independent of our own preconceptions. In this "otherness" of the subject we are drawn out of our isolated knowing into the community of troth; we are drawn out of merely knowing into being known.

Let me give some examples. I occasionally teach a course on "contemplation and action," which is rooted in the life and writing of Thomas Merton. Before I begin to deal with the conceptual and practical issues involved, I take time to introduce the class to Merton himself, with the care I would take in introducing one good friend to some others. I pass around photographs of Merton to give my students a visual image of him. I sketch out his biography, dwelling on moments of struggle and transcendence in his life. I hand out a collage of Merton's writings that represents his varied voices and have the class read it aloud, moving around the circle. I play a tape of Merton speaking to his students, so that my students can hear the sound of his own speech. I try in every way possible to allow my students to meet Merton the man—so that as the course goes on I can call on the objectivity and "otherness" of Merton's own reality to check and correct our private perceptions of the subject. The abstract subject of "contemplation and action" is thus grounded in the personal reality of Thomas Merton, and my students are invited into community with the subject through the person so that they can discover its personal reality in their own lives.

Another example. When I use the Buber story about the angel who wanted to change the world, I ask students not only to look at the world that story portrays but to put themselves in the midst of it, to enter into its dynamics and into dialogue with its characters. I do this by using a simple device. Once we have read the story and talked about it, I ask each student to write a continuation of the story in which he or she takes the place of the angel who has been told by God "that souls must be made fertile with flood and sorrow, that through them the Great Work may be born."

How does the angel respond to God? What does God say back to the angel? And what does the angel then do—slink away in despair, repair to private life, jump off a bridge, form a committee? After half an hour of silent writing time we share the results. Our insight into compassion deepens because we have been brought into a living relationship with the subject through a story about a world in which compassion is both necessary and painfully difficult. In writing and sharing their own extensions of the story, students find themselves becoming exposed and known.

The dialogue approach can be used in teaching a novel or a poem. Too often we ask students simply to view such pieces— sometimes not even with their own eyes but through the eyes of recognized critics. But a verbal creation is not meant merely to be viewed. It has a voice, not only the voice of its creator but the voice of the creation itself, a voice that can be interviewed. So let us bring students into conversation with these voices. Let the novel or poem speak to the student, and let the student put words into the poem's mouth, making it say things that are not there. Make the student accountable for showing what the poem actually says that evokes his or her response. And when the student has responded, ask him or her to listen for a counter-response from the voice of the poem itself.

Dialogue of this sort saves "objectivity" in the best sense of the word. The critic's voice is not truly objective; it is simply the voice of one more student who has tried to come to terms with the poem. It is also the voice of an external authority that speaks so loudly that the voices of other students and the poem itself can barely be heard. Truly objective knowledge comes as students and poem speak to each other in ways that allow the poem's voice to "object" to the students' response. If our task is to understand the poem, the most objective voice in the room belongs to the poem itself. We will hear that voice in part as various students report on what it says to them. But our ultimate aim in practicing obedience to truth is to allow the poem to speak of its own integrity, its own personhood. As Carol Bly says about the teaching of Mozart's music:

> Remember we are not now talking about you or yourself. We are talking about someone *other*—a musician long dead—and he is making a demand on us, and we are going to meet that demand![6]

Paradoxically, as we listen obediently to the voice of the other, our own speech becomes clearer and more honest; through the other we learn much about ourselves. For now we have been challenged by the most objective reality in the universe—a personal voice whose truth is related but not reducible to our own, a voice that knows us even as we come to know it.

We can help students enter into relationship with the "third party," the subject, not only in lecturing and discussion but also in their private and silent study. In the previous chapter I described the monastic practice of *lectio divina* or sacred reading. The purpose of this slow, meditative reading of brief texts is not only to create a space for learning but to bring the reader into obedient dialogue with the person behind the words. The contemporary monk Thomas Keating describes the process this way:

> Christianity is not centered around moral teaching, but around a person. . . . The Scripture is the normal way of introducing us gradually to the knowledge and love of this person. This process involves the kind of dynamic that happens in making friends with anyone. You have to spend time together, talk together, listen to each other, and get to know each other. At first you feel a little awkward and strange in one another's company, but as you get better acquainted, and especially as you feel yourself going out to the goodness you perceive in each other, the

amount of time spent in conversation begins to diminish. You are at ease to rest in one another's presence with just a happy sense of well-being.

The process I have spoken of in terms of human friendship is the way *lectio divina* works too. In a sense, it is a methodless way of meditation. It does not depend on some particular technique, but on the natural evolution of friendship. . . . It is a personal exchange.[7]

This same approach to reading, this quest for dialogue with the other, is found in Abraham Joshua Heschel's description of the way Hasidic Jews are taught to read the Torah and Talmud:

Torah study is a way of coming into the presence of God, the Baal Shem taught. A man learning Torah could feel like a son who receives a letter from his father and is most anxious to know what he has to say to him. The letter is precious to him upon every re-reading, as if his father stood there beside him.

Persuaded that one should be capable of learning more from people than from books, the Baal Shem sought to add a personality dimension to the study of the Talmud, a great part of whose contents consists of views of sages cited by name. He urged students to seek communion with the sages as well as comprehension of their ideas. Thus, it was maintained that, while learning "Abbaye said" or "Rava said" one should see Abbaye and Rava (as well as understand their utterance). One had to live with them, to enter their minds and souls, not just to grasp their thoughts.[8]

Students should be brought into dialogue not only with wise and congenial persons who can befriend them; there is equal value in dialogue with the enemy. To read the utterances of Adolf Hitler in this meditative style is to enter a relationship with evil. In this way we learn that evil is not simply "out there," in other persons and blind events. We touch the potential for evil in our own souls, and by our resistance to the evil in the other we may learn to resist our own.

One way to make this style of reading and its fruits more available to students is to ask them to put their dialogue on paper—to produce the sort of written conversation we have before us when we study the dialogues of Plato and Socrates. People who have no experience with writing out their inner dialogues suspect that the result will not be genuine conversation, but only the writer talking to him- or herself. But as we gain experience with the method, surprises begin to emerge. We find the other saying things that we did not anticipate and do not want to hear. We find the other challenging us in ways that are totally unexpected and unwanted. As we take the inner dialogue outside ourselves, making it public and visible to ourselves and to others, a remarkable degree of objectivity occurs. Again, we find ourselves exposed and known.

There is also a place for memorization in this form of teaching and learning, in this practice of obedience to truth. To "remember" means literally to re-member the body, to bring the separated parts of the community of truth back together, to reunite the whole. The opposite of re-member is not forget, but dis-member. This is what we do when we forget truth: we are dismembering the relationship between us and the rest of reality, between us and the knowledge we need to take our part in the community of truth. Memory allows us to enter dialogue with other beings who are distant in time and space. As our memory deepens and expands, our network of face-to-face relationships grows richer, more complex. We can call upon memory to introduce third parties, and more, to the present conversation, to invoke voices too distant in time or space to speak easily for themselves. By teaching students to re-member, and by inviting those memories into the classroom conversation, we recover the presence of the third party and find another way to practice obedience to truth.

Teaching and Friendship

Practicing obedience to truth in the classroom, practicing responsive listening between teacher, students, and subject, is not finally a matter of technique. It depends ultimately on a teacher who has a living relationship with the subject at hand, who invites students into that relationship as full partners. Here is the largest hospitality on which this sort of teaching relies: the hospitality of a teacher who has a fruitful friendship with the subject and who wants students to benefit from that friendship as well.

Students will often say that their favorite teachers are ones who are enthusiastic about their subjects even if they are not masters of teaching technique. More is happening here than the simple contagion of enthusiasm. Such teachers overcome the students' fear of meeting this stranger, this subject, by revealing the friendship that binds subject and teacher. Students are affirmed by the fact that this teacher wants them to know and be known by this valued friend in the context of a well-established love.

The metaphor of friendship helps identify some demands of this sort of teaching. The teacher, who knows the subject well, must introduce it to students in the way one would introduce a friend. The students must know why the teacher values the subject, how the subject has transformed the teacher's life. By the same token, the teacher must value the students as potential friends, be vulnerable to the ways students may transform the teacher's relationship with the subject as well as be transformed. If I am invited into a valued friendship between two people, I will not enter in unless I feel that I am valued as well.

The friendship metaphor does not mean that the classroom must be all sweetness and light. The true test of a friendship is its ability to sustain conflict, its capacity to incorporate tension as a creative part of relationship; indeed, it is in tension and conflict that the transformations of friendship often occur. The teacher who loves a subject must not try to force that love upon the students. The teacher, like any lover, must be capable of having a lover's quarrel with the subject, stretching and testing the loved one and the relationship. In this way students are invited into the negation as well as affirmation, into argument as well as assent, within the secure context of friendship and hospitality.

But the metaphor of friendship also alerts us to a common problem in teaching. The teacher may love the subject in a possessive way that prevents the students from entering in. The teacher may be so protective of the subject, and of his or her relation to it, that students are required to accept the subject on the teacher's own terms, discouraged or forbidden from assessing the subject and finding their own relation to it. Here, the teacher's enthusiasm is not an invitation but a demand. Here, truth is mistakenly thought to reside in the teacher's personal relation to the subject, and not in the widening network of relationships the community of truth requires.

The problem arises, of course, when we are fearful and insecure about our love, about our relationship with the other. We do not want that bond challenged or threatened; we become angry at anyone who either dislikes the object of our love or loves it more than we and wants to take it away. More than a few classrooms are constricted by this problem: the teacher is so possessive of the subject that students are denied the chance to relate to it on their own terms. Students may fall into line with such a teacher, do what the teacher requires, say what the teacher wants them to say. But under such a teacher, students do not practice obedience to truth, do not learn to forge a personal bond of troth with the subject and its world.

The problem is in the teacher. It is grounded in the teacher's insecurities and fears. It is one among many problems in this mode of teaching that can be solved only as the teacher pays attention to his or her own spiritual formation. "To teach is to create a space in which obedience to truth is practiced." But before we can teach that way outwardly, we must open a space for truth within ourselves.

7. The Spiritual Formation of Teachers

The Inward Transformation

> Some brothers . . . went to see Abba Felix and they begged him to say a word to them. But the old man kept silence. After they had asked for a long time he said to them, "You wish to hear a word?" They said, "Yes, Abba." Then the old man said to them, "There are no more words nowadays. When the brothers used to consult the old men and when they did what was said to them, God showed them how to speak. But now, since they ask without doing that which they hear, God has withdrawn the grace of the word from the old men and they do not find anything to say, since there are no longer any who carry their words out." Hearing this, the brothers groaned, saying, "Pray for us, Abba."[1]

With each word I have written for this book I have had the sense that Abba Felix was standing behind me, looking over my shoulder. His silent presence has not been comforting. It has been a continual reminder that words are not enough, that however accurate a teaching may be it is not truthful until we follow it with obedience. His presence has also been a silent rebuke, a reminder of all the times I have strayed from the guidance my own words offer. I have wondered when Abba Felix might break his silence and say to me, "There are no more words nowadays, . . ." bringing this flow of language to a sudden stop!

But I have also remembered some of my own advice, offered in Chapter 3. Writing about a time when words were taken from me because I failed to follow their leading, I said: "Seldom do we live up to the truth we are given, but that does not mean we must cease speaking the truth. Instead, we must be obedient to the whole of our truth—including our frequent failure to live it out. If we can do that, with ourselves and with each other, the words of truth will continue to be given, and we will be given the power to live them more fully."

So, another confession, offered in the hope that it might placate the spirit of Abba Felix: the way of knowing, teaching, and being I have described in this book is difficult and demanding. I often fail to follow it in my life and work, even though I am convinced it is a pathway toward wholeness. I am frequently defeated by forces within and outside of myself, forces that lead me to objectify and manipulate life even as I yearn for mutuality and (roth.)I must learn to resist those forces as Abba Felix did—with disciplines of spiritual formation that cultivate my capacity to practice obedience to truth.

Most teachers are well acquainted with the outward forces that defeat personal and communal teaching and learning. We have a long and groaning litany of complaints. Community has broken down in our schools, and competition is the norm. Objectivism reigns supreme, the unquestioned epistemology of most academic disciplines. Our schools and our students are better organized to ward off challenge and change than to open themselves to truth's transformations. Education is the slave of an economic system that wants to master and manipulate nature, society, and even the human heart in order to gain profit and power. So teachers who try to create a space in which obedience to truth is practiced must do battle with a host of external enemies.

Given such an analysis, it is tempting to survey some strategies for institutional change. Those strategies can be helpful—but not until we have done some inner work. For our tendency to blame institutions for our problems is itself a symptom of our objectivism. Institutions are projections of what goes on in the human heart. To ignore the inward sources of our educational dilemmas is only to objectify the problem—and thereby multiply it.

By the view of truth presented in this book, reality is not merely "out there," apart from us—and this includes the realities of educational institutions. Reality is "in here" as well, and therefore between us; we and the rest of the world conspire to create the conditions in which we live. So the transformation of teaching must begin in the transformed heart of the teacher. Only in the heart searched and transformed by truth will new teaching techniques and strategies for institutional change find sure grounding. Only in such a heart will teachers find the courage to resist the conditions of academic life while we work and wait for institutional transformation.

Our hearts have been deformed by our lust for power, by our fear of mutually accountable relationships, by our self-destructive tendency toward an alienated life. If we are to reform our teaching and our way of knowing the world, we must allow our hearts to be known by the love and truth in which they were first formed. We must practice disciplines that permit love and truth to re-form our hearts, disciplines that empower us to do the sort of teaching that can help re-form our students, our schools, and our world as well.

Some Spiritual Virtues

Before I explore some practical disciplines of spiritual formation, I want to describe some of the fruits of spiritual practice—humility and faith, reverence without idolatry, love and openness to grace.[2] I want to show that these classical spiritual virtues are epistemological virtues as well; the degree to which they are present in us has much to do with our capacity to know and be known in truth. They are virtues one can see in Abba Felix, virtues nurtured by a life of spiritual discipline that made him not only a person of God but a great teacher as well.

Humility is the virtue that allows us to pay attention to "the other"—be it student or subject—whose integrity and voice are so central to knowing and teaching in truth. Its opposite is the sin of pride, once defined by G.K. Chesterton as "seeing oneself out of proportion to the universe." In the words of Karl Deutsch, humility is "an attitude towards facts and messages outside oneself . . . openness to experience as well as to criticism . . . a sensitivity and responsiveness to the needs and desires of others."[3]

In humility, Abba Felix made space for his students and truth itself to speak. Had he been a prideful teacher, he would have rushed to answer his students' plea for "a word" with evidence of his own expertise; he would not have allowed their misguided request to stand there, in the open space, until it could be seen for what it was. It takes humility for a teacher to create and sustain silence, a silence in which we withhold the instant answer so the question can really be heard. The teacher who lacks humility will be unable to create a space for any voice except his or her own.

Humility not only creates a space in which the other can speak; it also allows us to enter into obedience to the other. In the silence Abba Felix created, he was reaching for obedience, trying to hear the reality behind his students' plea, wondering how to respond faithfully to it. If obedience means mutual subjection to the community of truth, it can never be practiced by a person who is "out of proportion to the universe." A prideful Abba Felix would never have acknowledged his students' power over him, the power to deprive him of the words of truth. He would have given them the wisdom they thought they wanted, words that would not have met their need to be called to account but only his own need for autonomy and dominance. A prideful teacher wants to subject students to his or her masterful self-image; writ large, this is the pride of our scientism which wants to enslave the universe to its objectifications. In humility we allow ourselves to know and be known in relationship, and in that allowing we draw our students into the community of truth.

But humility alone can lead to imbalance. It can create a teacher who is more open to others' voices than to his or her own, who defaults on the community by receiving but not giving, listening but not speaking. The spiritual life is lived in a balance of paradoxes, and the humility that enables us to hear the truth of others must stand in creative tension with the faith that empowers us to speak our own.

Abba Felix had this faith, or else he would not have been able to speak words that disillusioned and humbled his students. "Faith," says Karl Deutsch, "implies commitment to some judgment of our own. . . ."[4] Abba Felix possessed the courage of his own judgment. Knowing that troth between his students and their teachers had been broken, he refused to speak words of false comfort which would have satisfied his students but led them further from the relationship called truth.

Humility and faith taken together, Karl Deutsch writes, "offer us no model of a perfect working arrangement, but rather indicate the two boundary conditions between which a viable pattern must be sought."[5] The two in tension help us to know when to listen and when to speak, when to accept and when to resist, when to yield to the tuggings of the communal bond and when to tug back. There is no formula, no technique, that can guarantee this balance. It can only be sought and found in the heart made humble to others and yet faithful to itself through spiritual discipline.

The paradoxical balance of the spiritual life is revealed once more in the virtue of reverence without idolatry. "Reverence," writes Deutsch, "involves the refusal to pay more respect to the lesser than to the greater, or to the smaller than the larger context."[6] Abba Felix was a teacher who gave reverence where reverence was due. He did not attach ultimacy to his own small circle of students, did not pretend that what went on among them was unrelated to the larger reality. He gave his reverence to the greater community of troth and to its ultimate source. He showed his students how their disobedience had destroyed that community by cutting it off from its very source, saying, ". . . God has withdrawn the grace of the word. . . ." The desert teachers knew that the relations between themselves and their students were a microcosm of the larger truth they wished to teach, the truth of relatedness and obedience to ultimate reality. They gave their reverence to the larger rather than the smaller context.

The call to reverence always stands in tension with the injunction against idolatry, which continually questions what we give our reverence to. Idolatry, as Karl Deutsch points out, involves preferring the familiar over the infinite, the local over the universal, treating the former as if they were absolute.[7] Sometimes it is easy to spot our idolatries, as when we give our reverence to self or success or the nation-state. But there are more subtle forms of idolatry, made all the more dangerous by their subtlety. If we give our reverence to the community of nature and humankind but not to its transcendent source, we may appear to be reverent when in fact we are idolatrous. The same is true if we appear to give our reverence to that source when in fact we are attached to our conception of it.

Abba Felix's uneasiness about words was doubtless a result of his fear of idolatry. To live without idols is to live loose to all words, to devote oneself to the dynamic of relational truth rather than any frozen concept of "the true." The injunction against idolatry calls us beyond the fixed and finite reverences that language can create into the living experience of truth's community. Only as our reverence is continually tested for idolatry can we sustain the challenging dynamic of practicing obedience to truth; only in this tension will we be open to truth's transformations. The teacher who wishes to practice obedience to truth in the classroom must not give ultimate reverence to the words of self or students or subject. Such a teacher must revere only the living word that comes from that loving source who made us in community and continually calls us back to obedient life together.

Humility and faith, reverence without idolatry: these paradoxical qualities that allow us to teach truth are, as Deutsch says, "expressed with precision in the commandment 'Thou shalt love thy neighbor as thyself.' It is a command that at the same time indicates the twin opposites of love: self-abasement and self-idolization."[8] Abba Felix was filled with such love, I think—a love for himself that empowered him to speak his own truth, a love for his students that allowed him to risk a truth they needed but did not want to hear. Invoking the word "love" does not resolve the paradox, does not relieve the tension. But it does point us toward the source from which great teaching arises, the center that survives the tensions of practicing obedience to truth.

How do we touch that love, allow it to touch us? Perhaps it is by living faithfully within the paradoxes and tensions themselves, refusing to resolve them by collapsing into one pole or another, but allowing them to pull us open to that transcendent love in which all opposites find reconciliation. Such is the sug-

gestion of E.F. Schumacher, whose words about love I find not
only evocative but absolutely true to life:

> ... All through our lives we are faced with the task of reconcil-
> ing opposites which, in logical thought, cannot be reconciled.
> The typical problems of life are insoluble on the level of being on
> which we normally find ourselves. How can one reconcile the
> demands of freedom and discipline in education? Countless
> mothers and teachers, in fact, do it, but no one can write down a
> solution. They do it by bringing into the situation a force that
> belongs to a higher level where opposites are transcended—the
> power of love. ... Divergent problems, as it were, force man to
> strain himself to a level above himself; they demand, and thus
> provoke the supply of, forces from a higher level, thus bringing
> love, beauty, goodness, and truth into our lives. It is only with
> the help of these higher forces that the opposites can be recon-
> ciled in the living situation.[9]

When we do not allow divergent problems to pulls us open to
the power of love, we are unable to stay in the creative tensions
of the community of truth. We evade the demands of paradox by
clinging to one pole or the other—giving superior status to one of
the many voices rather than joining them all in conversation. We
may try to will the love necessary to see us though, but eventually our will falters and, wearied of the effort, we hold fast to a
fixed position and break troth with truth's complexities. For the
love that can see us through is not a product of our willful efforts.
It comes, as Schumacher says, from a level beyond us. It is, in
Deutsch's words, a gift of "grace."[10] By his refusal to flee from
the tensions of truth, Abba Felix brought his students beyond
their merely curious questioning into a sharp awareness of their
own need for grace: "... the brothers groaned, saying, 'Pray for
us, abba.'"

When mere curiosity is the source of our need to know, we
distance ourselves from truth; curiosity is a symptom of our need
to control and master truth rather than letting truth master us.
But when we pray for grace, we risk being invaded by a truth we
cannot control. The concept of grace, as Karl Deutsch suggests,
differs from curiosity "at this essential point. In terms of grace we

may regard information or events originating from outside ourselves as answers to our innermost problems of self-determina-
tion."[11] Openness to this sort of grace has been vital in the development of all knowledge. It has often gone by other names, like
"serendipity" or "flash of insight," but it is grace nonetheless,
breaking through our preconceptions and allowing truth to speak
to us.

Of course, the spiritual concept of grace goes beyond "information" and "events" into a realm of relational mystery that is at
the heart of the way of knowing and teaching described in this
book. In receiving spiritual grace we understand that we not only
seek but are sought, that we not only know but are known, that
we not only love but are loved. Indeed, it is *because* we are
sought and known and loved by grace that we are capable of
seeking and knowing and loving. The disciplines of spiritual formation aim finally at enlarging our capacity to receive this larger
grace, a grace that is always reaching for us from the heart of
love. It is a gift we cannot manipulate and command but for
which we can only pray.

The spiritual virtues I have explored here, which are virtues of
knowing and teaching as well, are alien to most professors today.
But the original and authentic meaning of the word "professor"
is "one who professes a faith." The true professor is not one who
controls facts and theories and techniques. The true professor is
one who affirms a transcendent center of truth, a center that lies
beyond our contriving, that enters history through the lives of
those who profess it and brings us into community with each
other and the world. If professors are to create a space in which
obedience to truth is practiced, we must become "professors"
again. To do so, we must cultivate personal experience of that
which we need to profess.

The Disciplines of the Academy

What Karl Deutsch says about grace can be said of all the spiritual virtues: "Such resources cannot be predicted but they can be
prepared for."[12] This is the function of spiritual discipline—to

ready us for the breakthrough of humility and faith, reverence without idolatry, and love and grace. What are the practical disciplines that can open us as teachers to receive these gifts in our lives?

First, I want to explore some practices already common in academic life. They are not usually thought of as "spiritual disciplines," but I want to show that they are in fact ways of preparing the inward space where we can practice obedience to truth. I hope to demonstrate that spiritual discipline is not as alien to academic life as it may sound at first.

One discipline is the simple practice of studying in fields outside one's own. It is no accident, I think, that great teachers often have wide-ranging interests that they bring to bear on the specialties they teach. The greatness of their teaching lies not simply in the fact that they can spice up their physics lectures, let us say, with illustrations that appeal to the musically minded, though that helps. More important, the expansive interests of these teachers create a spaciousness in their approach to their specialties as well.

As long as teachers stay within the safe bounds of their expertise, they can maintain the delusion of mastery. To know a subject too well, and not to venture into others, is to risk becoming closed to fresh insight in favor of familiar facts. But when a teacher is continually exploring alien, uncharted territory, humility and openness to grace are cultivated. That teacher is constantly reminded that he or she does not know it all, and the resultant openness of mind creates a space in which both students and subject can speak fresh truth.

A similar discipline is practiced when faculty are required to teach in fields outside their own, as in the undergraduate "common course" where economists must respond to poetry and poets must try to understand the new physics. When faculty teach outside their fields, they can no longer lecture *ex cathedra*. Now they must learn to listen carefully to a subject whose voice they are hearing for the first time, and to students who may have more insight into the subject than they themselves. Under these conditions, teachers are compelled to learn consensual methods of teaching and learning, of seeking and being sought by truth. Under these conditions, the spiritual virtues are not only encouraged but required for survival!

Teachers can deepen this discipline of standing outside their specialties by becoming students again. When they do, their minds are again broadened, that inner space for new knowledge is created without which one cannot create a learning space for others. But even more is happening when the teacher becomes a student in someone else's classroom—the spiritual discipline of "displacement" is being practiced. The teacher is forced to see the world from the student's point of view, to deepen that capacity for empathetic identification that enables us to practice obedience to truth. The result is more than new knowledge. It is the enlargement of our capacity for community, of our ability to receive the personhood of students.

Several times in my teaching career I have become someone else's student, and each time the experience has had a marked impact on my own teaching. I was forcefully reminded that education is not just a cognitive process, not just the transmission of facts and reasons. It is a process that involves the whole person, and so involves deep feelings as well. The feelings I remember most were frustration followed by boredom. The frustration came when the lecturer said something dubious but did not leave space for questioning, or when the class got into a conversation where the pieces did not connect, or when I began to realize that many of us, myself included, are far more gifted at speaking than at listening. The boredom came as my feelings of frustration were given no room for expression, forcing me to withdraw and tune out.

Through those experiences I realized the importance of creating classroom space for feelings as well as facts, of establishing an ethos of obedient listening where both facts and feelings can be expressed and responded to. Fresh from being a student I became more open and responsive as a teacher. But as those experiences receded, my teaching tended to drift back into old patterns that are self-centered and subject-centered but oblivious to the selfhood of my students. The discipline of displacement must be practiced regularly if it is to bear continual fruit.

The discipline of displacement can also be practiced in our research. I think, for example, of John Howard Griffin who studied racism in the United States not by detached data gathering but by darkening his skin with a chemical and traveling as a black man in the South. From his experience with taking the place of the other came the book *Black Like Me*, surely one of the most probing analyses of black-white relations we have.[13]

If Griffin's mode of research is too radical for most of us, we can still find ways to re-search the world by occupying the other's viewpoint. I think, for example, of Loren Eiseley, a natural scientist who spent hours and days and weeks immersing himself, imaginatively and sometimes literally, in the life of his subjects. He tried to see the world from the perspective of animals in evolution, of forests in transition, of streams and oceans changing shape and flow over long periods of time; his essay on floating down the Platte River allows us to feel the life of water itself.[14] Eiseley's legacy is a body of writing that brings us into community with the nature around us and in us, a way of teaching that calls us into the truth that is troth.

I suggest that certain "spiritual disciplines" are available to us among the accepted practices of academic life—if only we would see them and use them as such. The core academic activities of teaching and research offer us many opportunities to open the inward space in which we can practice obedience to truth—if we can learn to do them from the standpoint of "the other." Am I always teaching and researching within my specialty and never outside it? Am I always the teacher and never the student? Am I always studying my subject from the outside rather than from within? If so, that inward space will close down and my capacity for obedient relationship will diminish. But if I can step outside my subject and my role, however slightly, I will find my way further into the community of truth.

In Silence

The disciplines I have been exploring are primarily ways of opening our minds to new perspectives, new data, new interpretations. But the kind of knowing and teaching described in this book demand deeper disciplines, deeper openings. So I want to look at some of the traditional spiritual practices that reach beyond our minds to draw all our faculties, our total selves, into the mystery of relatedness.

These traditional disciplines aim at revealing the prerational ground of our knowing and our living, the ground of love from which truth arises. As such they are alien to many academics, not simply because they are not practiced, but because the prerational always contains the risk of irrationality which academics rightly fear. But if we would teach a truth whose totality is beyond the mind's capacity to capture or conceive we must risk disciplines that break the mind's dominance. As we do so, we will find that spiritual practice contains its own antidotes to irrationality. Even more, we will find our rationality enriched and expanded by the power of prerational love. The risk we feel is not really the risk of error; it is the challenge of transformation that comes as we allow ourselves to be mastered by truth.

Silent meditation is one of the most ancient spiritual disciplines, practiced by the desert fathers and mothers and all their contemplative decendents. In silence the rational mind wearies of seeking truth by main force and humbles itself to the truth that seeks us. The intellectual fruits that can grow in silence have been attested by Henry Bugbee:

> Philosophy is not a making of a home for the mind out of reality. It is more like learning to leave things be: restoration in the wilderness, here and now. . . . By "leaving things be" I do not mean inaction; I mean respecting things, being still in the presence of things, letting them speak.[15]

But when we begin to practice silent meditation, we often find ourselves in a wilderness where all things are mute. Our minds are so accustomed to telling things what they are rather than listening for their response that our early experiences with silence are often exercises in atheism, apparent proof that there is nothing waiting to talk with us. Louis Dupré writes about this sense of "absence" that overcomes the silent seeker. But he also writes about the paradoxical discovery of presence we may make if we enter that absence deeply enough:

> The mystics start their spiritual journey from within, and that is the only place where the [contemporary] believer *must* begin, whether he wants to or not. But a major obstacle arises at once, for what the believer encounters in himself is the same absence which surrounds him. His own heart remains as silent as the world of which the creatures have ceased to speak in sacred tongues. Yet it is precisely in this deliberate confrontation with this inner silence of absence that I detect the true significance of the believer's current surge toward a spiritual life. For only after having confronted his atheism can the believer hope to restore the vitality of his religion. . . . If fully lived through, the emptiness of one's own heart may turn into a powerful cry for the One who is not there. . . . Here, the very godlessness of the world is invested with religious meaning, and another dimension opens up in this negative encounter with a world that has lost its divine presence. Thus the believer learns that God is entirely beyond his reach, that He is not an object but an absolute demand, that to accept Him is not to accept a "given," but a Giving.[16]

Dupré's description corresponds to my own experience with silent meditation, which began some ten years ago in a Quaker meeting for worship. Here, people gather to sit in silence for forty minutes or an hour in a simple, unadorned room. Sometimes the whole time passes quietly; sometimes the silence is broken by speech that comes, as Quakers believe, from the Spirit moving in the speaker's soul.

I came to Quaker silence from a background of liturgical worship and religious study; my faith had been formed and sustained by words. At first, the silence was appealing, restful. But soon I felt anger and resentment over this sort of "worship." It seemed fraudulent to me in contrast to the reading and preaching of the Word. When we sat in silence I heard nothing, and when people spoke their messages often did not seem "religious." My anger finally built to the point where other members became aware of how I felt.

A few of them confronted my anger and helped me confront myself. They did not tell what to believe about the silence or about God but asked discerning questions that soon revealed the source of my feelings. I was angry because the silence forced me to face my own lack of spiritual experience; in silence I could find no personal grounding for the theological words and ideas that had been the foundation of my faith. I had a headful of notions about religious reality, but little direct experience of the reality itself. I had spent many years telling myself what that reality was like rather than listening for a voice that might defy all my concepts and theories. The silence made me angry because it forced me to listen—and all I could hear was my own faith crashing down around me.

With the support and guidance of my worshipping community I have been able to resist the temptation to turn back from this inward and silent journey to the comforts of received religious ideas. I have been encouraged to pursue the inward search more deeply, to journey on in the land of silence and absence. In doing so, I have begun to discover the God who is "not an object but an absolute demand . . . not . . . a 'given,' but a Giving." Today, ideas from religious tradition have begun to offer me guidance once more, as I realize that those who articulated them struggled in silence as I do. But if I use their ideas to define "objective reality," I default on their search and mine. Like them, I must sink in silence beneath all my definitions of truth to meet a truth that wants to define me.

My experience with silence may seem "religious" but utterly unrelated to the kind of knowing that concerns us in education. For me, that is not the case. My crisis of faith led me to question the whole structure of objectified knowledge. In the silence I have not only experienced God's absence—as God is defined by the objective language of creed and dogma; I have also experienced the absence of self and world—as they are defined by the constructs of objectivism. If we are faithful to the silence, we not only discover that God is no object. We also discover that we ourselves, other selves, and the creatures of the world are not objects either. To listen for the truth that seeks us, to hear it speak its own name, we must be silent not only in God's presence but in the presence of all we would know.

The skillful anthropologist does not rush into a village imposing the received concepts of social science on its people and life patterns. Instead, he or she spends much time in silent, receptive listening for the other's reality. The skillful literary critic does not first classify a novel as to "type" and then impose deductive categories upon it. Instead, he or she reads in a way that allows for silent, unobtrusive entry into that world, a participation in its dynamics that respects the balance of forces the novelist has achieved. Even in physical science the greatest advances seem to come in the silent way. Who was Albert Einstein if not a contemplative, the constant silent host to a nearly inaudible world whose whispers he alone could hear?

Louis Dupré describes this silent breakthrough to truth in terms that apply to our intellectual lives as well as to our spiritual experience:

> The spiritual person comes to view the world in a different perspective. Underneath ordinary reality he or she recognizes another dimension. At the very core of each creature, the contemplative finds an otherness that compels him to allow it to be itself and to abstain from the conquering, objectifying attitude we commonly adopt. This does not reveal a new idea of God; rather, it allows reality to reveal itself.[17]

When God and the world seem absent in silent meditation, we must not misinterpret the experience. What abandons us in silence is not reality but the objectifying mind-force we use to construct reality. In silence, the barriers of objective knowledge fall away. Because we have been mistaking those barriers for reality itself, reality seems to fall with them. But after a while we learn to receive reality anew. We learn to abstain from telling God and the world what they are; we learn to listen instead for their self-revelation.

In Solitude

The ultimate lesson silence has to teach is that God and the world have not absented themselves from us—we have absented ourselves from them. We have hidden ourselves behind the barriers of impersonal knowledge because we do not want to be found out. The knowing self is full of darkness, distortion, and error; it does not want to be exposed and challenged to change. It seeks objectified knowledge in order to know without being known. If we can learn this lesson from the discipline of silence, we will be led into the discipline of solitude where this evasive knowing self can be brought out of hiding to be transformed by truth and love.

If knowledge allows us to receive the world as it is, solitude allows us to receive ourselves as we are. If silence gives us knowledge of the world, solitude gives us knowledge of ourselves. The two disciplines are obviously related. If we are to receive reality as it is, we, the receivers, must be in good operating condition, well tuned and free of internal static. In solitude we discover and correct the self-distortions that prevent us from receiving God and the world as they are.

Solitude—a fundamental discipline of those fourth-century seekers who have been our guides on this journey—means not only the absence of other people. It means detachment, as far as possible, from our normal routines, reliances, and roles. Solitude calls us to confront ourselves with a directness impossible in everyday life, to learn who we really are and what we can rely on.

Solitude seems to contradict the call to community which has been so prominent in these pages. But solitude and community coexist as the poles of yet another paradox in the spiritual life. It is a paradox amply illustrated by the desert fathers and mothers who set out to become hermits yet ended up inspiring monasticism, the most durable form of religious community we have. Solitude opens us to the heart of love which makes community possible; life in community manifests the love we touch in solitude. Community requires solitude to renew its bonds; solitude requires community to express and test those bonds. If we live at one or the other pole of the paradox, we sacrifice either the inward content or the outward form of truth itself.

But most of us in our daily lives exist neither in solitude nor in community but somewhere in between. We sacrifice both the form and content of truth. Seldom are we truly alone, and seldom are we truly in relationship to others. This is the vacuousness of mass society and of mass education: our lives alternate between collective busyness and individual isolation but rarely allow for an authentically solitary or corporate experience. In this half-lived middle ground, our solitude is loneliness and our attempts at community are fleeting and defeating. We are alone in the crowd, unable to touch the heart of love in ourselves or to touch others in ways that draw out the heart.

Community, I have claimed, is the nature of reality, the shape of our being. Whether we like it or not, acknowledge it or not, we are in community with one another, implicated in each other's lives. But community is not the collective identity of the crowd that cancels out all selfhood. Nor is it a mystic merger into a single, cosmic self. Instead, it is a network of relationships between individual persons, solitary selves, each with an identity and an integrity. That self is all any of us has to bring to this community. If we are to bring our identity and integrity, if we are to bring our personal truth rather than a destructive package of illusions and lies, the discipline of solitude is essential. In solitude we come to know ourselves as we are, to know ourselves as we are known by love.

But the self-knowledge that comes in solitude does not feel loving at first. In fact, many people fear and flee from solitude because of what first comes with it—deadening boredom, then deeper inner darkness. That boredom contains a kind of self-knowledge, of course. It reveals how little we mean to ourselves, how much we depend on external factors for our sense of self and vitality. We rely on agendas, or on the role we play, or on the response we get from others for our identity, our very life. When these are removed by solitude, our liveliness disappears with them, and we experience that loss as boredom.

But if we stay with solitude, our boredom gives way to an even more devastating kind of self-knowledge. Deprived of external function and purpose, we can be engulfed by internal darkness, by a cloud of doubts and anxieties and guilts, of recriminations and resentments and regrets. Unhealed memories of the past catch up with us; unholy fears about the future crash in on us. In solitude we sometimes make the most difficult discovery of all— that we can barely stand to be in our own company!

No wonder the crowd is so appealing—it saves us from ourselves. In the crowd we can stay busy and distracted, avoiding the darkness within and projecting it on others. No wonder the crowd never becomes a community. It is composed of people who have not sought self-knowledge, people whose unexamined inner distortions inevitably distort their knowledge of and their relation to the community called truth.

In solitude we do not gain more knowledge about the world, about what is "out there," but we gain something far more valuable: knowledge of what is "in here," of who it is that knows. As we come to know the knower, to know ourselves, we come also to understand the liabilities and limits of our knowledge of the world. Dependent on external conditions for our identity, we often distort reality by making it a foil for our needs. Filled with fears and fantasies, we distort reality by projecting our own darkness on it. The entire objectivist agenda, which insists on locating all problems and solutions "out there" somewhere—solutions that often involve violent change in external arrangements—is rooted in our failure to come to terms with what is "in here" and between us. But as we face ourselves in solitude, we are slowly freed from the stranglehold of our dependencies and darkness and from the destructiveness of our objectifying life.

The freeing and healing discipline of solitude requires that we simply stay with it, confronting ourselves with patience, bearing the pain that comes as we withdraw our projections from the world and find their source in ourselves. As we do so, solitude eventually offers a quiet gift of grace, a gift that comes whenever we are able to face ourselves honestly: the gift of acceptance, of compassion, for who we are, as we are. As we allow ourselves to be known in solitude, we discover that we are known by love. Beyond the pain of self-discovery there is a love that does not condemn us but calls us to itself. This love receives us as we are. It creates a space in which we can let go of our self-delusions and allow ourselves to be transformed by truth. As we do so, we are better able to create a space to receive the world as it is, a space in which obedience to truth can be practiced.

In Prayer

Together, the disciplines of silence and solitude create the conditions for prayer, that basic spiritual discipline I defined earlier as the practice of relatedness. In solitude we acknowledge ourselves. In silence we acknowledge the world. In prayer we acknowledge the spiritual bonds that tie us and our world together. Prayer is the way of paradox—a way of entering into silence so deeply that we can hear the whole world's speech, a way of entering into solitude so deeply that we can feel the whole world's connections. In prayer we touch that transcendent Spirit from whom all things arise and to whom all things return, who makes all things kindred as they go.

It seems appropriate to end this book by speaking of prayer, since that is where the story of Abba Felix ends as well: "Hearing this, the brothers groaned, saying, 'Pray for us, abba.'" We do not know how Abba Felix responded to this petition, but it is tempting to imagine him quoting a passage from Paul's letter to the Romans (8:26–27, 29):

> We do not even know how we ought to pray, but through our inarticulate groans, the Spirit . . . is pleading for us, and God

who searches our inmost being knows what the Spirit means. . . .
For God knew his own before they ever were. . . .

So often we think of prayer as an act of intellect, a well-phrased message to God. If that is prayer, then everything depends on our flawed knowledge, on our frail capacity to articulate what we know. But the deeper we go into prayer, the more we realize that "we do not even know how we ought to pray." True prayer brings us to the edge of a great mystery where we become inarticulate, where our knowledge fails.

Abba Felix was a great teacher because he brought his students to this edge where all they could do was groan, revealing their remorse for having broken troth with their teacher and with the truths he taught. There is even more groaning today as humankind suffers the consequences of a way of knowing and doing and being that has broken troth with the community of creation. But these very groans, Paul says, are prayer. Even if we do not know what they mean, God does, for God knew us in our innermost being before we ever were. At the depths of prayer, reduced to guttural groans, we learn that even if we do not know how to pray, we are still being prayed in and through and for. We learn in prayer that when our words fail, we are still offered the Word, that when our knowledge fails, we are still known.

Once we have been to the depths of prayer, we can begin to know as we are known. Our prideful knowledge, with which we divide and conquer and destroy the world, is humbled. Now it becomes a knowledge that draws us into faithful relationship with all of life. In prayer we find the ultimate space in which to practice obedience to truth, the space created by that Spirit who keeps troth with us all.

Notes

Chapter 1

1. Transcript of *The Day after Trinity: J. Robert Oppenheimer and the Atomic Bomb* (Kent, OH: PTV Publications, 1981), p. 30.
2. Ibid., p.16.
3. Jonathan Schell, *The Fate of the Earth* (New York: Avon Books, 1892), p. 100.
4. Arthur Levine, *When Dreams and Heroes Died* (San Francisco: Jossey-Bass, 1981).
5. Ibid., p. 103.
6. Thomas Merton, *Love and Living* (New York: Farrar, Straus & Giroux, 1979), p. 3.

Chapter 2

1. On the relation of education to monasticism, see George H. Williams, *Wilderness and Paradise in Christian Thought* (New York: Harper & Brothers, 1962).
2. Fritjof Capra, "Buddhist Physics," in Satish Kumar, ed., *The Schumacher Lectures* (New York: Harper & Row, Colophon Books, 1980), p. 132.
3. Gary Zukav, *The Dancing Wu Li Masters* (New York: Bantam Books, 1979), pp. 31, 92.
4. Michael Polanyi, *Personal Knowledge* (Chicago: University of Chicago Press, 1958).
5. Richard Gelwick, *The Way of Discovery* (New York: Oxford University Press, 1977), pp. 77, 78.
6. Ibid., p. 82, emphasis added.

Chapter 3

1. E. F. Schumacher, *A Guide for the Perplexed* (New York: Harper & Row, 1977), p. 85.
2. Benedicta Ward, trans., *The Desert Christian* (New York: Macmillan, 1975).
3. Williams, *Wilderness and Paradise*.
4. Ward, *The Desert Christian*, p. 242.

Chapter 4

1. Schumacher, *A Guide for the Perplexed*, p. 39.
2. Ibid.
3. Ibid., p. 51.

4. Abraham Joshua Heschel, *A Passion for Truth* (New York: Farrar, Straus & Giroux, 1973), p. 45.
5. Jean Leclercq, *The Love of Learning and the Desire for God* (New York: Fordham University Press, 1977), p. 257.
6. Polanyi, *Personal Knowledge*, p. viii.
7. Herbert Mason, *The Death of al-Hallaj* (Notre Dame, IN: University of Notre Dame Press, 1979), pp. xviii, xix.
8. Margaret Mead, *New Lives for Old* (New York: Dell, 1966).
9. Loren Eiseley, *The Unexpected Universe* (New York: Harcourt, Brace and World, 1969).
10. Aldo Leopold, *A Sand County Almanac* (New York: Ballantine Books, 1966), pp. 239, 240.
11. An important discussion of personifying is found in James Hillman, *Revisioning Psychology* (New York: Harper & Row, Colophon Books, 1977), chapter 1.
12. Gelwick, *The Way of Discovery*, p. 9

Chapter 5

1. Ward, *The Desert Christian*, p. xx.
2. Ibid., p. xxiv.
3. Ibid., p. xxiii.
4. For the concept of hospitality, I am indebted to Henri Nouwen, *Reaching Out* (New York: Doubleday, 1975), chaps. 4-6.
5. From Howard Schwartz, ed., *Imperial Messages* (New York: Avon Books, 1976), pp. 113, 114.
6. Ward, *The Desert Christian*, p. 103.
7. Werner J. Dannhauser, "Leo Strauss: Becoming Naive Again," in Joseph Epstein, ed. *Masters* (New York: Basic Books, 1981), p. 259.

Chapter 6

1. Leslie Dewart, *The Future of Belief* (New York: Herder and Herder, 1966), p. 96.
2. Dietrich Bonhoeffer, *Ethics* (New York: Macmillan, 1978), pp. 367, 368.
3. Jay Hall, "Decisions," in *Psychology Today*, November 1979, pp. 51 ff.
4. Ibid., p. 86.
5. Ibid., pp. 52, 53.
6. Carol Bly, *Letters from the Country* (New York: Harper & Row, 1981), p. 38.
7. Thomas Keating, *The Heart of the World* (New York: Crossroad, 1981), pp. 45, 46.
8. Heschel, *A Passion for Truth*, pp. 63, 64.

Chapter 7

1. Ward, *The Desert Christian*, p. 242.
2. As the footnotes for this section indicate, I am deeply indebted to Karl W. Deutsch for his discussion of these spiritual virtues in *The Nerves of Govern-*

ment (New York: The Free Press, 1966), chap. 13.

3. Ibid., p. 230.
4. Ibid., p. 232.
5. Ibid.
6. Ibid., p. 233.
7. Ibid.
8. Ibid., p. 234.
9. E. F. Schumacher, *Small Is Beautiful* (New York: Perennial Library, 1975), pp. 97, 98.
10. Deutsch, *The Nerves of Government*, pp. 236–240.
11. Ibid., p. 237.
12. Ibid.
13. John Howard Griffin, *Black Like Me* (Boston: Houghton Mifflin, 1960).
14. Loren Eiseley, *The Immense Journey* (New York: Vintage Books, 1957).
15. Henry G. Bugbee, Jr., *The Inward Morning* (New York: Harper & Row, Colophon Books, 1976), p. 155.
16. Louis Dupré, "Spiritual Life in a Secular Age," in *Daedalus*, Winter 1982, p. 25.
17. Ibid., p. 28.

Index